How to negotiate with
intelligence, flexibility & power

WE HAVE A DEAL

NATALIE REYNOLDS

CEO of Negotiation Consultancy advantageSPRING

ICON

This book is for Leo. The most fearless, wily and persistent negotiator I know.

Published in the UK in 2016 by
Icon Books Ltd, Omnibus Business Centre,
39–41 North Road, London N7 9DP
email: info@iconbooks.com
www.iconbooks.com

Sold in the UK, Europe and Asia by
Faber & Faber Ltd, Bloomsbury House,
74–77 Great Russell Street,
London WC1B 3DA or their agents

Distributed in the UK, Europe and Asia by
TBS Ltd, TBS Distribution Centre, Colchester Road,
Frating Green, Colchester CO7 7DW

Distributed in the USA by
Publishers Group West,
1700 Fourth Street, Berkeley, CA 94710

Distributed in Australia and New Zealand by
Allen & Unwin Pty Ltd,
PO Box 8500, 83 Alexander Street,
Crows Nest, NSW 2065

Distributed in South Africa by
Jonathan Ball, Office B4, The District,
41 Sir Lowry Road, Woodstock 7925

Distributed in India by Penguin Books India,
7th Floor, Infinity Tower – C, DLF Cyber City,
Gurgaon 122002, Haryana

Distributed in Canada by Publishers Group Canada,
76 Stafford Street, Unit 300
Toronto, Ontario M6J 2S1

ISBN: 978-178578-032-5

Typeset in Sentinel by Marie Doherty

Printed and bound in the UK by Clays Ltd, St Ives plc

Contents

Introduction

This isn't like most negotiation books. Yes, we will talk about theory and process, but that's only a small part of what this book is all about. This book is designed to demystify negotiation and to teach you how to negotiate with intelligence, flexibility and power.

It doesn't matter who you are or what your background is. This is a book for anybody who negotiates. And so that's everyone. Negotiation is the most important skill in business, and in life, to get what you want, need or deserve. Are you doing what you can to get the best deal, every time?

From an unspoken interaction in the street with a stranger as to who will go first through the revolving door, to a strained conversation with a family member about what you want to do at the weekend, to a haggle with a car dealer, to a mediated contract and pricing dispute ... we negotiate all the time. It's a social lubricant. It's what keeps societies functioning, marriages working, businesses operating and countries interacting. Negotiation matters and as human beings we have been doing it since the dawn of civilisation.

I want to show you that negotiation is not a mystical

talent that requires extreme intellect, copious charm or buckets of experience (although those things can all be useful). The ability to negotiate is a skill that can be learned by anyone. Through identifying your strengths and weaknesses, learning the processes and mastering the tools, you can start to negotiate more effectively in all parts of your life.

And as with most things in life, practice makes perfect. I always think that it helps to view negotiation as being like a muscle. If you never flex or use that muscle, and you are then called on to run a marathon – perhaps view the marathon as a salary negotiation in this context! – then it's going to be supremely painful and a shock to the system, as you won't be at all prepared. If, however, you have used that muscle just a little bit every day, when the time comes for the marathon (or salary negotiation), you will be that bit more prepared and far more able to cope, and it will be much less painful.

This book is designed to give everyone the knowledge, skills and insight they need to be a brilliant negotiator in all aspects of their life. Whether you are negotiating with your partner, the boss or a supplier on another continent, whether you are new to negotiation or a seasoned pro, this book will give you what you need to up your game and be the best negotiator you can be.

PART ONE

Getting Started

CHAPTER ONE

Why Negotiation Matters

People negotiate all the time. We just don't always realise that we could be doing it, should be doing it, that we *are* doing it, or indeed how to do it well.

From the renegotiating of terms with a new client to the difficult conversation about missed performance targets with a supplier; from the request to your boss to have your role re-evaluated to the demanding of a lower monthly fee from your broadband provider, almost every interaction in which we are requesting something from someone else is a negotiation.

Some negotiations in life are more obvious than others. When my team works with delegates in our workshops, we will always ask them to imagine all the people they might negotiate with over the course of a day, week, month or year.

Let's start with the most obvious people who come to mind when you think of 'negotiation' – the people you work with most closely. What kinds of negotiation might you engage in with them?

Colleagues: Who delivers the difficult message to the boss? Who does what work, gets what desk or pays for the coffee?

Boss: You're likely to negotiate on a number of issues, from salary to promotion, job title, who's on your project team, time off and deadlines.

Suppliers, customers, partners or clients: You might negotiate about price, risk, volume, deadline, guarantees and performance indicators. These are what I would call 'obvious negotiations'; you may even note them in your diary as '2pm negotiation with client'.

But we negotiate in our personal lives too ...

Salespeople, estate agents and service providers: Outside of work you are likely to engage in negotiations with the suppliers of services or products to you or your family. Examples might include deliberations over the sale price of a new dining table with the furniture store salesperson, trying to agree a speedier completion date for a house sale with your real estate agent or seeking a lower tariff with your energy supplier in exchange for not moving to one of their competitors. Interestingly, many people wouldn't view buying furniture as an opportunity to negotiate, they would just pay the price on the ticket, whereas others will take great delight in trying to secure a discount, no matter how small. Similarly, some people will never really question the tariffs set by their energy companies and will simply sign up without really considering what could be changed or improved in the standard package.

Of course, a competitive and heavily populated market for energy supply should provide all of us with the incentive to push back and negotiate for better terms. Quite simply, if a provider says 'no', it is now easier than ever for us as consumers to find someone else who can provide what we are looking for. Similarly, I once ran a training programme at which one of the attendees was a sales director for a well-known high street furniture retailer. She explained that if a customer ever paid the ticket price for a product at their stores, the salespeople would think they were a fool. Why? Because the salespeople were mandated to offer an immediate 10 per cent discount if asked for one. If the customer demanded more, they would then 'reluctantly' go to 12.5 per cent. If the customer still wanted more, they could speak to the manager who in most cases would 'reluctantly' offer a further 5 per cent. In short, the discounts are often there to be had and are factored into the list price; you just have to ask for them.

Partner: On an almost daily basis you will have cause to negotiate with your husband, wife, girlfriend or boyfriend. This might be in relation to holiday plans, childcare arrangements, financial contributions or who will do the washing up.

So, I start most mornings (particularly on very cold, wet and windy days) by turning to my husband and saying: 'If you walk the dog, I'll get Leo ready for nursery.' (Leo is my toddler; you'll hear more about him in a moment.)

What's important about the proposal I've made to my husband? It's a trade. Why does the fact it's a trade matter? Well, quite frankly, it's because I don't want my husband thinking I'm going to do everything for him. He has to do something in return. The interesting thing is that we often readily trade based on 'If you ..., then I ...' with friends and family. The problem is that we don't tend to carry that through to our professional lives. Later on in this book, I'll tell you why that is one of the biggest mistakes we can make at the negotiation table.[1]

Wider family: We also have to negotiate with wider family members, such as our parents, siblings and extended family over issues such as allowance, curfews, family celebrations and which distant relatives you have to invite to your wedding.

Around August every year I will also start the annual negotiations with my mother-in-law about where we are spending Christmas that year. (This has become much more challenging since our son arrived in the position of first grandchild!) This leads us nicely on to the most effective negotiators.

Children: Those of you who have spent any substantial amount of time around young children will know that they are master negotiators.

I told you I would come back to my toddler ... He is an amazing negotiator. Not because I have taught him, but because children *just are*. The reason for this is because they focus all of their efforts on achieving the desired result (be that second helpings of ice cream, a new toy, watching one more episode of a cartoon, staying up late ...), and they will do pretty much anything it takes to get that result.

My team have trained negotiators in big companies around the world, and one of the things that we are frequently told by nervous negotiators is that they are scared of 'pushing too hard' when they negotiate in case people don't like them. Whereas, the interesting thing about children as negotiators is that, up until about the age of seven or eight, they don't really care that much about what people might think of them. It's only when we approach our teens that we start to become more self-aware and concerned as to how we might be perceived by others. So, until that happens, children will focus purely on getting the result that they need to 'succeed'. For my son, this includes stamping his feet, throwing things on the floor and screaming; because of this it's not uncommon for him to succeed in getting what he wants, particularly if we're in a busy public place!

Now of course, the advice here is not to stamp your feet and scream every time you get to the negotiation table. I'm not convinced that is going to help you bag that promotion or salary increase. But what we can learn from children is that sometimes we should think more about what we need to do to get the result, rather than dwelling too much on what people might think about us. I am not advocating that you shouldn't care at all about whether people like or loathe you; as you will see in Chapter Five, this can have an impact on the outcome of your negotiations. But it shouldn't be the only thing you are concerned about. You still need to have the right facts and information at your fingertips, the ability to stand firm, and almost certainly the confidence to say 'no' in order to get the right result. In short, you need to get the balance right.

We might be familiar or experienced in negotiating with all of these groups, but we haven't yet looked at the most challenging of negotiators, the one we have to face alongside every other counterparty.

Ourselves: Ladies and gentlemen, I would like to introduce you to the little voice in your head. The little voice in your head is the forgotten party in many negotiations, and yet it has the ability to derail the most prepared and intelligent of people. It can make you sell yourself short, lose your confidence or assume you are in a far weaker position than you really are.

It's easy to recognise that little voice. It often sounds something like:

> *'Don't ask for that, it sounds greedy.'*
> *'You can't go that high.'*
> *'You don't really know what you are talking about do you?'*
> *'They will never agree to that.'*

I routinely work with clients who are smart, intelligent

people, who have studied the facts, numbers and details, and who have a plan for how they want to negotiate; yet as soon as they get to the negotiating table that little voice kicks in and preys on their stress and anxiety. And it's amazing how regularly people are swayed by it. They hear it and panic; then they ask for less, offer more or don't bother asking at all.

We all have that little voice in our heads. Whether you are young or old, male or female, recent graduate or CEO. It's there. It's just that the voice speaks so loudly to some people that it clouds their judgement, erodes their confidence and ultimately prevents them from negotiating as effectively as they could.

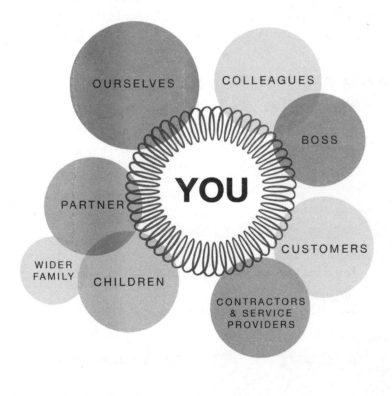

How do you stop yourself from being a victim of the little voice in your head?

1. Get to know your little voice. One of the most powerful ways to combat that little voice is simply to recognise it's there! By accepting and recognising its existence, you have already taken away some of its hold over you, as it is then less likely to be able to pop up and derail you unexpectedly.

2. Listen to it. Try listening to what the little voice is saying. Reflect on the messages you hear in your head when you are in a high-stakes or stressful negotiation. Annoying and limiting as that little voice is, it also reflects your inner concerns, apprehensions and fears. By simply writing down what that little voice says to you at high-pressure moments, you can prepare to fight back next time.

3. Counter it. Once you have identified the negative messages, you can start to build robust responses. If in preparing for a salary negotiation that little voice whispers, 'They will never agree to that figure', or, 'You're not worth that much', use this insight to your advantage by researching why you *are* worth that much or what other employers are paying for your level of expertise. We are most vulnerable when we haven't prepared or don't have supporting information, so listen to the fears being voiced in your head, and then go and find out all the information you need to answer back.

4. Drown it out. So much of effective negotiation is about confidence. Negotiation can be challenging, awkward and uncomfortable, and this impacts our performance. One tip is to start to drown out the negative messages before you even get to the negotiation table. Before that little voice is able to kick in, take the time to tell yourself what you really want to hear: that you are valuable, worth it, well prepared, confident, compelling ... and keep telling yourself that.

5. Recognise they have one too. Guess what? It's not just you who has the little voice. Your counterparty does too. And their little voice is whispering to them about their pressures and anxieties. A smart negotiator realises that if all they focus on is their own little voice then they are missing a huge opportunity to tip the balance of power and gain valuable insight as to the key issues in the negotiation. While doing your research, take the time to think about what the concerns and fears of your counterparty might be. By understanding those, you can use the information to your advantage. Check out the next chapter to find out more about this.

This gives you some insight into just some of the negotiations that happen in our lives. We'll get into the details of how to negotiate with each of these counterparties later. First, let's demystify the idea of negotiation itself.

When my team are training businesspeople on how to negotiate, we use the following definition:

'Negotiation is two or more parties discussing differences in order to try to reach an agreement.'

We use this definition because it is broad and not too prescriptive.

First, notice that the definition does not mention money. There is no reference to pounds, euros, dollars or yen. We do this very deliberately because we don't want you to think that the only negotiations that matter are the ones relating to cost, fee or price. Not everyone will negotiate on financial matters all the time. Indeed, some people may never negotiate on those things. Some people might negotiate on risk, deadlines, volume, policies, positions, points of view, politics or location, and they just won't be exposed to financial negotiations. These negotiations are no less important or influential in our lives. We should not be dismissive of negotiations just because they don't contain discussions on mega-bucks.

Secondly, this definition does not present boundaries as to what negotiation might look like. There is no one 'type' of negotiation, just as there is no one type of counterparty. We negotiate a great number of different things and as a result our negotiations can 'look' very different. A negotiation could look like you and me having a conversation over a coffee. Or it could look like a multi-party, multi-variable, cross-jurisdiction, politically sensitive, disputed contract renegotiation. And everything in between.

Thirdly, this definition of negotiation makes reference to the fact that *you might not reach agreement*. Not all negotiations end in a handshake or a signature. Some negotiations will end in deadlock, dispute or a very pleasant acceptance of the fact that the numbers just don't add up on this occasion.

So, we begin this book by being clear that negotiation is a fundamental part of what it is to be human. It's the skill that is going to allow us to get what we want, need or deserve because, despite the old saying, good things don't always come to those who just wait ... and wait ... and wait. You need to take the initiative, be in control and ask.

What's the problem?

Despite the fact that we negotiate every day, the reality is that many of us don't really like it that much. Many people will find it awkward, uncomfortable, time-consuming and cringeworthy.

Even the most confident and intelligent people will experience uncertainty and fear at the prospect of going into a negotiation. Their hearts will beat faster, their guts will start churning, panic will set in, and as a result they will often underperform or avoid negotiating altogether. (In Chapter Two, I will explain why the avoidance strategy is not a sensible one.)

The potential long-term cost of not negotiating

Whether it's down to fear and nerves, not wanting to look 'greedy', reassessing the profitability and desirability of the deal, or worrying about whether you have the time, people will choose not to negotiate for a number of reasons.

In certain situations you might choose not to negotiate because you figure the uplift you might be able to achieve doesn't warrant the discomfort or potential reputational risk of negotiating for more. However, you would be wise to exercise caution when adopting this approach. Take the example of negotiating your salary. Imagine that 35-year-old Tom has just received a job offer from a company that he is really keen to join. The salary they have offered Tom is £100,000. As this seems like a reasonable figure and as he doesn't want to look greedy or difficult, he accepts. On the same day, 35-year-old Imogen, who is equally qualified, is offered the same role within the same company, for the same £100,000. However, Imogen chooses to negotiate her salary and is able to secure an additional £6,500, taking her starting salary to £106,500. Let's say that each applicant stays at the firm for 30 years, each receiving a 4 per cent pay increase annually. If Imogen decides to retire at age 65, Tom would need to work for an additional six years to be as wealthy as Imogen at retirement, all because of that additional 6.5 per cent when they first joined the firm.

Despite it being a fundamental requirement of human existence and interaction, negotiation is one of the few skills that the majority of us are never really shown how to do well. Yes, you might have taken a module at college or university, or on an MBA course; or your boss may have told you to 'watch and learn' as they negotiated deals. The problem is that a lot of these courses are very abstract and theory-driven and don't serve us that well in the 'real world' (which was certainly my experience when doing legal training), or that our well-meaning bosses are actually just teaching us their bad negotiating habits or asking us to emulate a style that might not work that well for us as individuals.

This book is all about bringing together the elements of both people and process when it comes to negotiation. I will help you to make sense of the academic theories and studies, learn how to master the tools and tactics and understand how knowing yourself, your preferences, behaviours and feelings will allow you to take control of your negotiations and come out on top.

Let's begin.

CHAPTER TWO

Common Negotiation Mistakes

I t may seem like a counterintuitive place to start, but looking at some of the most common mistakes people make at the negotiation table can help you to become the best negotiator you can be. The mistakes in this chapter can result in us agreeing far less productive, robust, sustainable and profitable outcomes, both for us as individuals and for our employers. By working to avoid these mistakes, you will strengthen your chances of being able to walk away with the best deal. I'm going to be really explicit about what not to do, so that you can see at a glance whether you're guilty of falling into some of these common, deal-limiting traps.

These mistakes are made by negotiators regardless of their age, experience, seniority, location, gender or culture. My team and I have seen these mistakes being made again and again at the negotiation table.

It is really important that negotiators of all levels realise two things.

1. **It's not just you making these mistakes.** We see them being made by negotiators the world over. If you recognise that you are making some of them, don't think for a moment that you're inferior to your peers. The reality is they are probably making these mistakes too ... you just haven't realised it until now.

2. **Experience doesn't make you immune** – indeed it can sometimes make you more vulnerable! It would be very dangerous for a more experienced negotiator reading this book to think that at this point they can skip ahead to the next section. Even seasoned deal-makers can benefit from a scrutiny of their skills and performance every now and then. It's really easy to slip into bad habits when negotiating and we believe that by making a few small changes most people will be able to see some improvement in the results they are able to secure.

As you read this chapter, try to recognise these mistakes in both yourself and others. Think about times when you might have committed these errors: what led up to them, and what did they cost you? What might you have gained had you done things differently? Then commit to wiping them out of your negotiations for good!

Mistake One: Thinking negotiation is all about winning

It's a fact of life that human beings want to win. It's a natural urge to want to come out on top, to thrive and be the best. We have *had* to be competitive in order to survive. Yet interestingly, I meet lots of people who tell me that they are not at all competitive.

Really? Let's just think about that. When was the last time you woke up, got out of bed and thought: 'You know what? Today I really want to lose, to be second best, to come out not quite on top'?

I thought not. The simple reason is that human beings want to succeed and, ultimately, to win. This book will help you do that when you are at the negotiation table. But the first mistake many people make is to assume that negotiation is all about winning. Which it isn't. Not outwardly anyway.

Wanting to win, rather than wanting the other party to lose

Let's be clear. I am not advocating the approach of: 'I want to win, therefore I don't care at all about whether you lose.' Having a desire to get the best result you can doesn't make you selfish, nor does it mean you have to act selfishly. The desire to be successful can co-exist with a concern for others. Later in the book we will be exploring an approach to negotiating which allows you to do just that.

Of course, you should always try to get the best possible outcome you can when negotiating. You should want to win. What you shouldn't do is actively advertise any victory to your counterparty. By this I mean you should avoid a huge grin, a pat on the back to a colleague or even a fist pump, if you're that way inclined. Don't let your counterparty see that you are delighted with the result. Why? Because nobody likes to be made to feel or look stupid.

How do you think your counterparty is going to feel after witnessing your obvious elation? They are probably going to feel annoyed, embarrassed, frustrated, resentful and angry. They might still sign on the dotted line or shake your hand, but they will be the customer or client who never pays their invoices on time, never recommends you to anyone else, always questions your judgement, always asks for more output for less cash. They will do this because human beings hold grudges. They will remember how you made them feel and will try to get even.

Instead of celebrating your victory, try making them feel like they have won. Ensure that they are satisfied with the deal. Even if you have just got the deal of a lifetime, you should be smart enough to temper your elation, keep your jubilation inside and be quietly satisfied that you have got what you need and more. You shouldn't need the spectacle of a victory dance to feel like you have come out on top.

A word of caution here. When trying to make them feel satisfied, don't take it too far, or it will be just as obvious as your victory dance. If you have just concluded a negotiation with someone and they then praise *your* performance and eulogise about what a great deal you have done, beware! They are probably trying to make you feel better about the fact that *they* have just walked all over *you*!

Mistake Two: Thinking you can avoid negotiating altogether

You may have felt a pang of recognition at the negative, intrusive thoughts of the 'little voice inside your head'; or, when you think about negotiation, you may have a more physical response: gut churning, heart pounding, feeling awkward and uncertain. On the other hand, you may experience no fear but feel frustrated that the whole process can be slow and time consuming. You may also think that the negotiation process is damaging to the trust or relationship you have been able to develop with a client or customer. As a result of some or all of these factors, you may actively try to avoid negotiation.

We regularly observe clients going to great lengths to limit the time spent negotiating or attempting to bypass the process entirely. In an attempt to hurry things along or reach some kind of agreement as quickly as possible, we hear them using phrases such as:

> *'Let's cut to the chase.'*
> *'Give me your best number.'*
> *'Let's talk real numbers, shall we?'*

If you recognise this as something you do – *stop*. You might think that this strategy is benefitting the overall deal or the relationship, but it isn't.

The reason for this is that negotiation is a necessary ritual. It isn't a bureaucratic invention of the boardroom; it's something we have been doing for millennia. It's a social lubricant, an essential part of how things get done and how we co-exist in the world. It allows for friendships and marriages to grow, children to be educated, businesses to prosper, societies to function and countries to collaborate (and in all these cases, sometimes the alternative). Negotiation is such a key part of what it is to be human that we can't pretend it doesn't exist.

So, the next time you think you can preserve your nerves, protect the relationship or speed things along by shortcutting the negotiation process, remind yourself of these three important points:

1. People like to be given the chance to get the best deal they can for themselves, and if you deprive them of that, they won't thank you for it. The negotiation process is a chance for each side to explore just what might be possible in that deal. It is their opportunity to ask questions, consider alternatives, uncover risk, check they have considered all options and carry out their own form of due diligence. If you deprive them of that opportunity, then you might find that the following point will start to cause you problems.

2. If you make the negotiation too easy (either by taking shortcuts or bypassing negotiation altogether), the other side will start to question why. You might think that by avoiding negotiation, they will be grateful.

But in most cases the opposite is true. They might be happy with their expedited or easily won outcome for a time, but ultimately doubt will surface. What have they missed? What's wrong with the deal? Have you misled them? The little voice in your head we encountered in the previous chapter will speak up and start to question just why the deal was so quick and so easy. It's when this begins to happen that deals and agreements can become vulnerable to being revisited, renegotiated or even rejected completely.

3. It is essential to understand that people generally value the things they have had to work hard for. And this is also true at the negotiation table. Remember when you were young and you had to save weeks and weeks' worth of pocket money to get your hands on a new pair of trainers or a concert ticket? When you finally got that item you treasured it as you understood just how hard you had worked or saved in order to get it. Well, this is also true when we negotiate. If we have had to work hard to trade with the other side, explore alternatives and craft a clever solution that works for everyone, we will feel far more satisfied with the outcome.

So don't try to avoid negotiation. Whether it's for reasons of fear, nerves and anxiety or a misguided attempt to speed things up, avoiding or limiting the negotiation process is likely to only lead to two outcomes. The first is that you deprive yourself of making the most of opportunities that come your way, and the second is that your counter-party starts to question your motives and the quality of the deal that you so readily agreed to.

Negotiation is a part of who we are. Rather than speed it up or avoid it altogether, simply learn how to play the game. Ultimately your career, bank balance and counter-parties will all thank you for it.

The no-negotiation doubt trap

Imagine you are looking to buy a new car and you have a maximum budget of £5,000. You have been looking at online advertisements for private car sales, and after a long period of failing to find what you are looking for, you finally see a seller close to where you live offering the model you want for £5,000.

You call up the seller and arrange to meet her the following day at her home to take a look at the vehicle. The following morning when you arrive at the seller's property, she shows you the vehicle and takes you out for a test drive. After only five minutes you start to think just how much you like the car and how much you would like to get it. Fearful that you are going to miss out but keen to get the best deal you can, at the end of the test drive you say to the seller: 'Look, I like the car very much. I'm going to cut to the chase here and make you an offer for your car. The price I'm offering you is £4,000.'

Imagine that the seller puts her hands on her hips, takes a breath and then says, with her hand outstretched to shake yours: 'Thank you very much. We have a deal! Nice doing business with you.' As you walk home to arrange finalising the transaction, how are you feeling?

The reaction I inevitably get when I pose this dilemma to clients is typically: 'I should have offered less!', 'It was too easy!', 'There must be something wrong with the car', or 'It was overpriced in the first place'. Some people, however, will say: 'I just got my ideal car for £1,000 under the asking price. What's not to like?' My response to those people is always the same: you might well think that. But trust me when I tell you that in about twelve to eighteen hours' time, that little voice in your head will kick in, and it will start to make you doubt or question why the seller so readily accepted your 'ambitious' price of only £4,000. What have you missed? What's wrong with the car? What does she know that you don't? You might even start to wonder whether you should go back to renegotiate or whether a handshake is legally binding. All of a sudden, your elation can devolve into dissatisfaction.

Mistake Three: Thinking great salespeople are automatically great negotiators

Whether we are selling a product, a service or ourselves as a subject matter expert or the perfect candidate for a job, in the business world the ability to effectively sell your position, point of view or product and convince someone to 'buy into' your vision or way of doing things is a hugely valuable one.

It is true that in the commercial world we are often

expected to sell and negotiate in quick succession. An example of this would be going to visit a potential client and selling your services over the course of a pitch, and then immediately after or a few days later, negotiating with that client the potential terms of any deal or relationship.

The potential problem here is that many people confuse the very different skills of selling and negotiating, and use them at inappropriate times or to such a degree that they undermine their position. It's useful to think about it like this. When we sell we will use different skills and behaviours compared to those we should use when we negotiate.

When we sell

When we sell we are seeking to *persuade* the other side of the value of our service or product. We will *explain* the benefit of what we have to offer, *justifying* why our offering is superior to our competitors' and explaining in great *detail* and with huge *enthusiasm* why our view is the correct one. We might *list all of the benefits* to be had by agreeing to what we are suggesting and may find ourselves *arguing* with the other side if they tell us what we have to offer isn't their best option. We will also *seek permission* and *consensus* with statements such as:

> *Can I send you further information on that?*
> *Would you like to hear more?*
> *Do you think this would work well for you?*
> *Does this price sound OK to you?*

When we negotiate

When we negotiate we should be seeking to *gather information* because, as you will see later in this book, information is power. Negotiators should ask *exploratory* and *insightful questions* to understand the motivations of the other side. Negotiators should be *firm, clear* and *concise* when communicating with the other side and delivering proposals. Negotiators should listen, so they can hear anything they might have missed or that could influence the deal. A negotiator should *control the interaction* because if they won't, the other side will. Negotiators should remain *calm* and *composed*, and *will carefully consider* all of the available evidence. And ultimately a negotiator should *propose firm options, rather than asking permission* from the other side.

You might think that some of the behaviours and examples in these sections would be beneficial to both a salesperson and a negotiator. For example, the negotiator's behaviour of gathering information would be also be useful to a first-rate salesperson. Similarly, the salesperson's behaviour of being enthusiastic can also be used to great effect by a negotiator. The difference lies in the emphasis placed on these behaviours in the two skillsets.

> **Salespeople** seek to establish a need or desire for what they have to offer
> **Negotiators** seek to create terms for an agreement once need or desire is established.

Of course, as I mentioned earlier, you might have to play

the dual role of salesperson and negotiator. In these situations, it is essential that you understand when to sell and when to negotiate.

Some people start to negotiate too early. Why is this an issue? If you start to negotiate too early – e.g. when you haven't completed the selling process and perhaps haven't fully convinced the other party of a need or desire – then you run the risk of coming across as presumptuous.

Some people will revert to selling too late. Why is this an issue? This is potentially the more serious of the two errors. If you start to sell when you should be negotiating the terms of your agreement or contract, you can end up sending a message of desperation and vulnerability to the other side.

Selling too late

Imagine that you are looking to buy 1,000 staplers for your company. You have been speaking on the phone to a stationery supply salesperson and you have listened to his sales pitch about the quality of his staplers. Acknowledging that you are interested in his product and are in the market to buy 1,000 units, you agree to meet at your office to look at settling terms. The pair of you start to negotiate an agreement for unit price and delivery, and you are quite happy with where things seem to be going.

After about fifteen minutes you propose a 'final offer' to the stapler seller. He responds by saying: 'You know, these are really quality staplers. Absolutely first rate. Look at the quality! Surely you can see the value in investing in a robust product such as this. If you recall, I mentioned earlier we also won an international innovation award ...'

How does that salesperson sound? Well, quite simply he sounds a little bit desperate. By reverting to 'selling' when he should be negotiating terms, he sounds like he is frantically trying to persuade and remind us as to the value of his proposition, which is likely to frustrate us and to make us question either the terms or the quality of his product.

It pays to ensure that once you start negotiating with your counterparty, you refrain from returning to selling behaviours. If you do return to selling behaviours, you run the risk of sounding like you are trying to remind everyone of the value of your offering, perhaps because you are desperate or vulnerable. Of course, it can be useful to engage in selling at the start of a negotiation, but keep it brief and focused before moving on to receiving, reviewing and making proposals, and closing your deal.

How do you know when the selling stops (or should stop) and the negotiation has begun (or should begin)? The answer is simple: you can't possibly start to negotiate until all sides have put their opening proposal on the table. Until then you don't know what the boundaries are of the issue you are negotiating, or the starting point of each side. Until then you also may not know whether the other side(s) are interested in trying to reach an agreement. It's only at this point that you can fully understand the scale of the task before you and can then start to negotiate and look for a resolution. Everything before that point is important and can influence the outcomes, of course, but, thinking back to our definition of negotiation on page 12, you're only negotiating once you know and can discuss each side's differences in order to try to reach an agreement.

Mistake Four: Not knowing who you are really negotiating with

We often make the mistake of thinking that the person we are sat opposite at the negotiation table is the person actually pulling the strings, making the decisions and steering the negotiation. This is the traditional view of negotiation, but, on many occasions, this is not the case.

Instead, the reality is that there will often be many interested parties in the form of bosses, board members, shareholders, members of the public, family members or other nations who have a vested or keen interest in the outcome of your negotiation. The person sat opposite you may in fact be answerable to a whole bunch of other people and is therefore, in many ways, merely the messenger.

It's important to map out these key players and string-pullers, because if you haven't factored in what success or failure looks like to the people in the background, then you may find it far harder to reach an agreement. Your proposals are going to need to convince or meet the needs of these people just as much as they need to convince the person sat in front of you. Professor Lawrence Susskind, who directs the MIT–Harvard Public Negotiations programme and co-directs MIT's Negotiation Pedagogy Initiative, refers to this process of mapping out hidden players as knowing your counterparty's 'back table'. A clever negotiator will map out the back table before they get anywhere near the negotiation.

The 2015 Greek 'bailout'

Over the summer of 2015, a series of high-profile negotiations were played out on the world stage. The political leaders of Greece were involved in high-pressure, high-stakes negotiations with the leaders of the other countries that make up the European Union. The negotiations centred on how Greece would pay back its EU creditors and manage its crippling national debt, and whether it would stay part of the single currency, the euro.

The negotiations were led by a number of top political figures from the Greek government, the EU and the International Monetary Fund. However, those influencing the outcome of those negotiations didn't always have a direct seat at the negotiating table. The proposals being made by each side were heavily influenced by public feeling across Europe, political parties in each side's home country, political leaders from outside Europe, global business leaders and international trade bodies. In Germany, the taxpayers were very firmly holding their chief negotiator, Chancellor Angela Merkel, to account. A negotiation will often have many more parties than those with a physical seat at the table.

TRADITIONAL VIEW OF A NEGOTIATION:

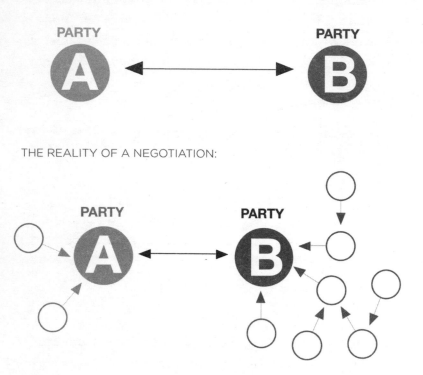

THE REALITY OF A NEGOTIATION:

Mistake Five: Thinking all negotiations are the same – and that they're all a battle

It may sound incredibly obvious or patronising when I say that not all negotiations are the same. But one of the most common mistakes that people make is failing to identify the type of negotiation they are engaged in. This diagram is a simplified version of the one my company uses on our workshops for business clients around the world. You will see four different types of negotiation highlighted on the graph: haggling, hard bargaining, trading and working together.

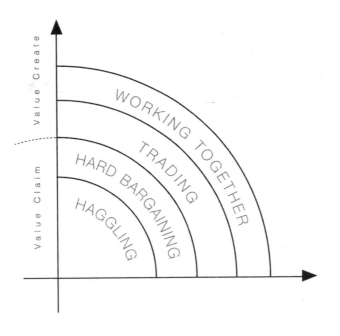

Haggling: This is the crude end of the spectrum. This interaction will probably be focused solely on each side trying to get the best possible price, as this is likely to be the only issue up for negotiation. It is likely that each side will have very little regard for how the other side feels, as they will never have to engage with that person again. Because of this, you might feel able to offer what could be viewed as 'extreme' price proposals. You will probably find it easy to walk away if you don't get the deal you want, as there will be little consequence and plenty of other options.

Example: going to Morocco on holiday and attempting to haggle down the price of a leather belt or a leather handbag.

Hard bargaining: This is the next step up from haggling and is still very transactional in nature, in that you are unlikely to have that much regard for any future relationship with your counterparty. Price will probably still be one of the most important issues for negotiation but there will probably be additional factors over which you can negotiate. While this interaction might take longer than a 'haggle', you can still walk away and look elsewhere if they don't offer what you are looking for.

Example: negotiating with a salesperson in the local mobile phone store over your new contract. You might be concerned with price, but also the handset you get, the length of the contract and additional 'extras' you can get to sweeten the deal.

These two examples of haggling and hard bargaining are what we would call **'Value Claim'** negotiations. This is because each side is looking to try to claim as much value as they can for themselves, normally with little regard for how this will affect a future relationship between the two parties. Value claim negotiations are often inherently competitive in nature.

Trading: This is about recognising that each side probably has things the other side would benefit from. You are likely to be negotiating on a number of different issues, such as fee, length of contract, time of service delivery or type of product. It may involve working together over a longer period of time, which will influence how you engage with each other and your concern with preserving a decent working relationship.

Example: You are looking for a contract cleaning company to come in three times a week to clean your firm's offices for the next twelve months. You have something the cleaning company wants: money and the ability to award a long-term contract. And they have something you want: high-quality cleaning services deliverable on a regular basis.

Working together: This is the antithesis of haggling and will involve two parties being dependent on each other's products or services and working together over an extended period of time. The variables on which you might negotiate could run into the hundreds, particularly if the situation requires greater integration between the two parties. The variable list might include logistical decisions, like office locations, pay and conditions, performance indicators, cost of contract, governance arrangements, make-up of the senior team, budgets, IT and infrastructure, and so on. In these situations it will be far harder to walk away, and each side will have a vested interest in ensuring that a positive relationship between the parties.

Example: a local authority outsourcing some of its back-office functions to a private sector firm for a ten-year period. In order to do this, they might create a new jointly owned company in which they are both invested. To facilitate the agreement they will have had to agree a huge number of variables.

These two examples of trading and working together are what we would deem to be **'Value Create'** negotiations. This is because the circumstances around the negotiation require each party to have the interests of the other side at the forefront of their mind in order to ensure maximum value. When you are in a negotiation that requires you to collaborate over a period of time, it makes sense for the parties to look at ways in which they could increase opportunities and potential value. Creating more value will often work well for both sides, as such Value Claim negotiations are often inherently more collaborative in nature.

When I explain the different types of negotiation to various audiences, some people usually say that, while this is all very interesting, in their line of work they just don't do the 'tough stuff'. They would never haggle with a client or hard bargain with a customer, as they engage in more long-term, collaborative engagements and interactions with the people they work for and alongside.

My response? I'm sure that is true in the vast majority of the negotiations that you do. But just because you don't have to do something often, doesn't mean that you will never find yourself in this kind of negotiation and that you shouldn't know how to do it well. In fact, I would suggest that it's all the more important that you know how to do it well, as you have probably had far less time to think about it or to practise it.

As we have explored, lots of people find negotiation difficult, uncomfortable and challenging, and this is only heightened when we are faced with a negotiator who behaves tough, goes for the jugular and seemingly won't back down. In those circumstances, when confronted with unsettling and potentially derailing behaviours, it is even more important that we are able to feel strong, prepared and confident about how we are going to handle the situation. (See Chapter Ten for tips on dealing with negative behaviours and barriers at the negotiation table.)

It might well be the case that you engage almost exclusively in more collaborative negotiations. You might have spent the last three years engaged in productive meetings and negotiations with your counterpart based in a company that is a customer of your organisation. You get on really well, you talk about your holidays, hobbies and family, and approach your negotiations with a collaborative mindset, looking for new ways to add value and further your relationship.

But imagine that all of a sudden, your regular counterpart moves on. Due to a change of strategy on cost efficiencies and rationalisation, the person that replaces your old counterpart has been selected because they are not afraid to be tough. They have been given the specific mandate to cut costs. At all costs. And they are not afraid to be tough, direct and unfriendly. How will you react to this? Are you prepared?

Similarly, even in the most collaborative of negotiation relationships, there will always be bumps in the road. From a bad-tempered argument with your other half to an accusatory and heated conversation between two partners in a commercial joint venture over missed performance targets, there will always be situations where, even though you plan to be in it for the long term and the relationship is generally good, there are challenging exchanges, heated debates and differing opinions to manage. Sometimes in order to get a resolution to a difficult issue you might have to have a firm, direct and awkward conversation. The skill in those situations, of course, is to know how to have that tough, direct, one-off conversation, while afterwards also being able to preserve and move the relationship forward in a productive and collaborative way.

Seduced by the language of partnership

The other aspect of this is that sometimes we are completely duped and misled as to the type of negotiation we are actually entering into. We need to be wary of allowing ourselves to be seduced by the language of partnership.

For instance, you might think that you have a great relationship with a potential customer. They seem interested in your proposition and have requested numerous proposals about how you might work together in the future. They invite you to their offices and offer you refreshments, you enjoy a long chat about your kids and the forthcoming holiday period, and then you sit down to talk business. As the conversation progresses, you become optimistic about the future potential, as this customer is talking about partnering, embedding your product into their workforce, joint development and global roll-out. They mention that they think your firm is a 'good fit' for them, that they are keen to grow and that they would like to take you with them on their journey. Wow. This is great!

Then you get down to the detail and start talking about the possible terms for any supply agreement. You outline your proposition and associated fees, and your potential customer, still smiling, says something like:

'You know we really are serious about wanting to partner with you, so for this first order could you just knock off twenty per cent to show commitment?'

'We love your product! Tell you what: if you can agree to discount this order, or maybe give us free delivery, we can make sure all our future orders are a lot bigger.'

'We are really excited about working with you going forward, but if you could just look at where you might be able to offer us better pricing, it will help us move forward with all the other projects we want to do with you.'

Because you are so excited and swept up in the idea of the future potential of this partnership and collaborative opportunity, you say yes. You agree to terms less favourable to you on the promise of future orders from them. Their talk of you being their preferred supplier or expansion partner means that you go easier on them – why wouldn't you? If you are going to be working together on a number of projects in the future, you want them to think that you are serious about the partnership and your relationship with them. Right?

But stop and think for a second. How often do the promises of future work, bulk orders and partnership agreements materialise? Have promises of preferential terms the next time you negotiate ever come to pass? Have you seen customers like this again at all?

Of course, in some instances their partnership talk is genuine (you can learn in Mistake Eight how to ensure that it's not just you who is giving), but you also need to stay alert to the times when there is actually very little substance to what the other side is promising.

We are all seduced by the talk of opportunity, partnership and relationships because it's what we want to hear. It sits more easily with most of us than having to be tough, direct and uninterested in the person we are negotiating with. But this can be dangerous. There are a lot of people out there who know that if you believe in the possibility of a beneficial partnership or collaboration you will go easier on them, providing preferential terms or improved pricing. So, they churn out convincing 'fake partnership' talk, even though they never intend to repay the favour, place the repeat orders or work in partnership.

So, how do you protect yourself? How do you know which type of negotiation you are really in?

The Five Factor Test

The Five Factor Test can be used to gain an indication of the type of negotiation you are in. You're looking not just for the presence or absence of these factors, but the extent to which each factor exists in your negotiation. As a rule of thumb, all of these factors exist at low levels in haggling but will gradually increase as you move through hard bargaining, trading and working together negotiations.

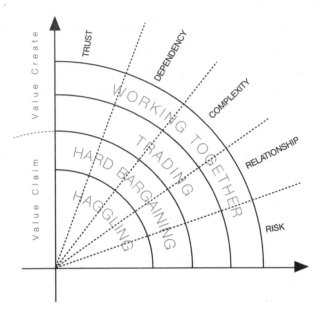

If you want to establish the type of a forthcoming negotiation, you can use the diagram above to plot the level of each of the Five Factors: trust, dependency, complexity, relationship and risk. Using the diagram, simply mark an 'X' in each of the five sectors, closer into the centre of the axis (bottom left) if the negotiation is low in that factor, and further away from the centre if the negotiation is high in that factor. You will find that Value Claim negotiations are more likely to have most crosses in the bottom left-hand corner of the axis, whereas Value Create negotiations are likely to have most crosses towards the top outer edge of the diagram.

Imagine that you are on holiday and you start to negotiate with a stallholder over the price of a leather belt. In that negotiation:

- There is no real demonstrable level of **trust** between the parties. Why would there be?

- The level of **dependency** is low as you can easily buy a similar item from another stall nearby and there is no formal agreement of any kind nor any need to use each other in the future.

- The **complexity** level is low as the only real issue you are negotiating over is price.

- There is no **relationship** of substance between the two parties.

- The level of **risk** if you overpay for the item or can't reach a deal is minimal.

Plotting this on the diagram clearly shows us that this is a haggling negotiation.

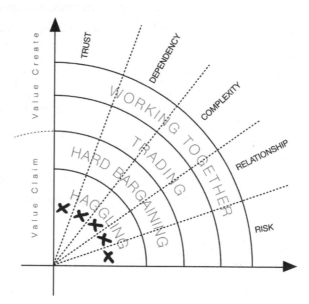

But if we now jump over to a negotiation discussing a ten-year joint venture between two companies, the Five Factors look very different:

- A solid level of **trust** has to exist between the parties in order for the venture to succeed.

- Each party is **dependent** on the other for this to work. Plus you are likely locked into a pretty complex legal agreement which means you can't just up and leave. And how many other parties could deliver exactly what you need for this deal right now? Dropping your counterparty is likely to have severe implications.

- In a deal like this there are likely to be multiple issues, in fact possibly hundreds. These could include issues such as contract length, governance arrangements, office location, logo, price, staffing, quality control ... As a result the **complexity** level is going to be high.

- The ongoing **relationship** is probably going to be so key that there will probably be dedicated Relationship Managers on each side of the deal.

- The **risk** associated with this deal failing? Potentially huge both financially and in terms of reputation.

Plotting this on the diagram clearly shows us that this is a working together negotiation.

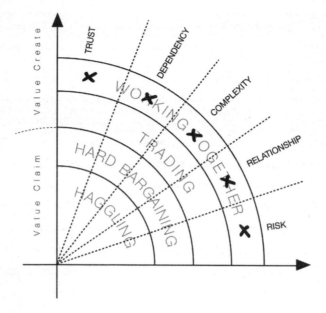

Undertaking a quick assessment of the Five Factors can start to give you some real insight into the reality of the negotiation you are in, but of course it is *just an indication*. If you had assumed you were in a very collaborative negotiation but upon examining it you realise that the other side have been wanting to only talk about price (low complexity) and are giving no firm commitments to future business (low dependency), then maybe you need to rethink how you need to approach it. We call this 'identifying your outliers'. Outliers are the areas in a negotiation that seem to not quite tally with the other factors you have identified on the Five Factor axis. If you identify outliers, you should consider how to address these issues when planning for the negotiation.

Outliers

You may find yourself in a situation where the negotiation appears to be a classic hard bargaining, competitive situation. Imagine that you are looking to buy a product as a one-off. You have identified a supplier locally; the only issue that will be up for negotiation is the price; you will have no need to work with the supplier again; and you have no existing relationship to preserve.

This would seem to warrant crosses low down on the axis. However, in this situation the consequences of you not securing the product in the next 24 hours are grave. It is imperative that you get this product. In this case, the risk and dependency crosses could be far higher up the axis.

These outliers will require you to think about how best to contain and manage the potential issue. Would you be willing to reconsider price in order to ensure a timely delivery? Or would it prompt you to take additional steps to identify an alternative supplier if this one cannot guarantee the delivery speed you need?

So as you can see, it is essential that you 'know your negotiation' before you get anywhere near the negotiation table. Make sure you have understood whether you are planning for a Value Claim or a Value Create negotiation and use this information to help you plan your tactics, strategies and behaviours. If you are unsure as to the type of negotiation you are in, try using the Five Factors diagram to get some insight.

Mistake Six: Never changing or adapting your style of negotiation

This mistake is very much linked to the previous one and concerns the reluctance of some people to flex or adapt their style when at the negotiating table. As we have seen from the previous section, there is no such thing as a standard negotiation. Each one is different and as a result requires a difference in your approach.

Many of us will have our preferred negotiation style. Around the world I have met a great many good cops, a great many bad cops, lots of relationship builders and plenty of ball-breakers. It's certainly not a bad thing to know your strengths and to play to them if you can. The issue is if you are unable to ever deviate from your preferred behavioural style, regardless of the negotiation, using it in situations that would benefit from a difference in approach.

How does this look in practice? In the previous section we talked about the different types of negotiation that you might be expected to undertake at different points in your life or career. It might well be the case that you are more regularly exposed to more short-term, direct, competitive negotiations. As a result, over time, you may have developed your tough guy style particularly well. Because you know that your tough guy style seems to get you what you need, you use it every time you negotiate. But imagine what would happen if you rolled up to one of the preliminary conversations regarding setting up a joint venture agreement (like our example on page 43), being tough, direct and uncompromising. The relationship and trust between the two potential partners in the room would no doubt be soured and could negatively impact the negotiations.

Alternatively, it could be that your industry tends to be involved in more long-term, collaborative relationships with customers or suppliers. As a result, you may have honed your empathetic style in such a way that it always seems to deliver the results that you need. You may come unstuck if you start talking about partnership, growth, collaboration and opportunity to a stallholder selling bags or trinkets in a foreign bazaar. If you did that they would be rubbing their hands in glee at the prospect of all the money they were going to make out of you.

Of course, these are exaggerated examples, but the fact remains that the ability to move between behavioural styles is going to be incredibly useful throughout your negotiating career.

Take a step back from your work environment for a moment. In our broader lives we know that sometimes we are going to have to be tough, direct and decisive, and other times we are going to have to be more thoughtful, collaborative and understanding. We seem to understand and implement this concept in life generally, but for some reason a great many people report feeling uncomfortable about doing it professionally. (In Chapter Eleven I explore why this is perceived to be a particular problem for female negotiators.) The main reason for this tends to be a fear of lacking credibility or authenticity if you were to regularly change your style. You may be concerned with being seen as disingenuous or worry that people will 'see through your act'.

People seem to have the most issues with playing it tough. The thing is, most of us will always retain an element of discomfort and awkwardness at having to stand firm, reject people and play hardball. This type of 'style' or behaviour is often the furthest removed from how we like to live our lives and how we would like our everyday interactions with others to be. But sometimes life calls on us to stand up and say no, to be louder, more forceful, stronger or more assertive. That doesn't mean we have to change who we are forever, but we might have to modify the behaviours we adopt for a limited time in order to get the result that we need. The trick is to do it as credibly and professionally as you can and in such a way that your nerves and discomfort don't limit you or trip you up.

Use protection

When I was studying at Bar School, I was given a wonderful insight by one of my advocacy tutors. A retired judge, he was a quiet, calm and charming man who was incredibly approachable and interested in the progression of others; yet he had enjoyed an almost fearsome reputation while on the bench for his no-nonsense style and directness. I remember one day asking for his advice. I had been struggling with some of the exercises that required us to be forceful, assertive and at times (I had felt) almost overbearing to those we were questioning. I asked him how he had been able to 'flick into' court mode so readily and so utterly convincingly. He said that the trick was to 'use protection'.

He went on to explain that when entering the court-room he knew he needed to project a certain style in order to be respected and taken seriously, and yet he also knew that this style was quite different from the person he was at home and in his personal life. So, in order to allow him-self to play the role of a tough, no-nonsense judge, he would see his robes as his protection. His belief was that in putting on his robes he was putting on a suit of armour that would protect the person he really was inside, while also allowing him to project whatever he needed to in order to get the job done.

After he was finished playing the role of tough judge, the robes would come off and he could go back to being the quiet and unassuming person who just wanted to see his grandkids and get home in time for tea. We dis-cussed how this same approach was also often adopted by people in the uniformed services, such as police offi-cers or security guards.

Of course, not all of us have physical robes or a uniform that we can put on before a negotiation, but we can all borrow the principle of using protection. Next time you go into a negotiation, think about what you could use to help you project the behaviours you need to temporar-ily, while preserving and protecting the 'real you' under-neath. Some people might carry a certain briefcase or wear a pair of shoes that gives them confidence. But it doesn't have to be an actual physical item; it could just be that you 'put the item on' mentally. Some people will refer to 'putting on their jacket', some to 'putting on a certain hat'. Whatever works for you, use it.

Alternatively, if you really struggle with this, why not take someone along with you who can play the role credibly and assign them to the task. A good example of this would be a married couple in which one spouse loves to haggle but the other finds it cringeworthy. So, when shopping for furniture or a new car, they can each play a role. One might have a list of questions and requirements lined up, but when it comes to the nitty gritty of price, their partner will take over. Or in a business setting, you might make sure that your negotiation team has a member who is more than happy to say no. If this is a strategy you would prefer to adopt, just don't fall into the trap of being an overly obvious good cop/ bad cop comedy act!

Mistake Seven: Trying to get too comfortable

As we have already mentioned, negotiation can be uncomfortable. Not for everyone and not all of the time, but a large number of people will go to great lengths to avoid negotiation because of how it makes them feel. Because so many people think of discomfort as a negative thing that they want to stamp out, they imagine that the optimum place to be as a negotiator is one where you are relaxed and stress-free. Stop! This is a dangerous approach. We need to recognise that negotiation is inherently uncomfortable and that, actually, by embracing the discomfort and learning to live with it, you will be a far more effective deal-maker. In short, negotiation isn't, and *shouldn't be*, a walk in the park.

The negotiators I train who most concern me are the ones who claim they have 'been there, done that' and have negotiated so many times that there is no need to worry too much about it. As a result, they take less time to plan and prepare, and end up going into every negotiation limiting the possible outcomes they might be able to achieve.

Negotiation is a very active and engaged skill. You need to be fully aware of everything that is going on around you. You need to be reading your counterparty; listening to what they are saying and how they are saying it; and watching them for clues, messages and hidden opportunities. You need to be mindful of what you are saying and doing, and what messages you are giving to those you are negotiating with. It's important to be alert in a negotiation so that you can be flexible and adaptable.

Police raids

I spent a number of years working alongside officers in London's Metropolitan Police early in my career and had the pleasure of working with some really experienced and interesting officers who had amazing stories and insight to share about human nature and the extremities of people's behaviour.

I recall speaking to an inspector who was responsible at the time for dealing with an escalating drug problem on a housing estate. As part of the Met's campaign to address the problem, they were conducting a large number of raids on houses known to be dealing drugs and allowing drug use on their premises. This inspector told me that when they were planning a raid, they didn't worry about the more junior, inexperienced officers who were nervous and asked lots of questions. Instead, they were concerned about the experienced 'old-timers' who felt they had done this kind of thing so many times that they didn't have to worry about it. His view was that the new recruits would listen carefully to instructions, think carefully about what they had learned in training and remain focused throughout, making them a sharp, observant and reactive support on a challenging operation.

Nerves can work in your favour. They can keep you sharp, alert, focused and receptive. Of course, that's only if they don't completely take over and limit your ability to perform. You need to get the balance right. Parts Three and Four of this book will equip you with the knowledge and insight you need to find that balance.

Put simply, we need to accept that negotiation can be uncomfortable. All the advice in the world won't change that from being the case. But this knowledge can help you to manage that discomfort. Or, put another way, negotiators should follow the mantra of the US Navy Seals and: 'Get comfortable with being uncomfortable!'

Mistake Eight: Giving things away for free

When we negotiate we tend to get fixated on achieving one or two things that are of great importance to us.

Those things might change from negotiation to negotiation, and they could be factors such as price, deadlines, volume or contract lengths. Understanding what matters to us is an important part of effective planning and of defining in advance what success at the negotiation table would look like.

However, the danger is that when we become so fixated on achieving that one super-important thing, we keep giving lots of other seemingly unimportant things away. The consequences of this strategy, incentivising or seeking to desperately persuade your counterparty on a particular point can be that you end up walking away with far less value or even in a weaker position than you were in the first place.

Beware freebies

My team were contacted to provide fee negotiation training to a global professional services firm. When we were conducting our pre-training research with the firm, we were given insight into why they might be experiencing 'profit margin erosion'. We discovered that eighteen months prior to our appointment, the divisional director at the firm had informed all fee-earners that there was going to be a new target hourly rate for certain pieces of advisory work. The target rate was set at £400 per hour. The staff were told that if they didn't consistently secure this figure, it would have a knock-on effect in their performance and pay reviews.

As a result, the fee-earners had this figure seared into their brains. It was all they thought about, all they could see. As a consequence, when they went to visit clients to try to win work, they would make the proposal of £400 an hour and then, in order to secure that amount, they would throw in all sorts of incentives and freebies, such as training, project management software, additional partner time, junior staff on secondment and speedier completion. At the end of the negotiation, they would get their £400-an-hour fee, but the cost of everything else they had given away meant that the overall value associated with the deal was hugely diminished, and their profit margin had shrunk as a result.

So how did we help the professional services firm to resolve the problem? And how can you avoid falling into the same trap? Once we got them to understand that their current approach was leaking value, we simply introduced them to the following phrase:

> *If you do this for me, then I can do this for you.*
> *If you ..., then I ...*

'If you ..., then I ...' is probably the most powerful phrase in negotiation and has been advocated as an approach by a number of experts in this field. It can help you to ensure profitability, sustainability and overall value. By phrasing all of your proposals this way, you help to preserve the value of the things you have to offer, you stop undermining your position and you see an increase in your bottom line. You can start to unlock and use the value in all of the possible trading variables. This is because when you ensure that you are only making concessions conditionally (that is, you are getting something from them in return), you are not just giving and giving and leaving your larder bare. By getting something back that you value, you are able to replenish your position.

It works on another level too. It conditions your counterparty to see that you are more than happy to help them achieve what they need, but that they are going to have to work for it. They are going to have to offer you the things you want in order for them to access the things they want. Decide now to stop giving and giving and giving. Instead, start to trade.

Take and give

In this section we have looked at how, in a negotiation, it can be useful to make it clear that you are willing to help the other party get what they need, but that you need to get what you need too. To me this goes back to pretty basic social conditioning around the value of working in order to get a reward, which is why I prefer the flipped expression 'take and give', rather than the more commonly used 'give and take'.

I was recently trying to teach my toddler, Leo, that he would only get his favourite sweets if he was a good boy and kept his playroom tidy (as he had recently become adept at emptying hundreds of tiny pieces of Lego all over the floor and then refusing to clean them up). As part of this process I explained to Leo that *if* he tidied up his bedroom, *then* I would give him a chocolate. I do it that way round so he understands that he has to do the task before accessing the reward. If I had tried to do it the other way round and presented the chocolate first, he would have grabbed it and run before I could even mention there was also a requirement to tidy his room!

Mistake Nine: Thinking it's all about you

This mistake is very much linked to the previous one. The problem is that we tend to think things are all about us. And I hate to break it to you that in relation to negotiation, they certainly shouldn't be. When we start to think about negotiating, we also start to think everything that really matters to us: our issues, our priorities, our fears and our successes. We become fixated on them, and they act like blinkers beyond which we can't ever really see. This is a problem because it means we miss opportunities that may exist in the negotiation but that just happen to fall outside of what we have deemed important from our perspective.

In a 2008 study, leading negotiation academics Galinsky and Maddox talked about the idea of 'getting inside your counterpart's head' at the negotiation table. The study showed that seeing things from the perspective of your counterparty is one of the most powerful ways to influence the outcome of your negotiation.[2] Why is this the case?

It's essentially because you aren't the only one at the negotiation table who has pressures, stresses, strains, deadlines and priorities. Your counterparty does too. And all of those things that might matter to them could present you with some real opportunities. But if you are too stuck inside your own head, thinking only about the issues and priorities that matter to you, you may not even see or anticipate that they have something going on which you could use as a lever to change the course of the negotiation.

People negotiate with people. You need to get inside their head to see the world through their eyes. How do things look to them? What do they hope to achieve? What does failure look like to them? Why are they here? What motivates them? The more we know about their fears, successes, priorities and ambition, the more we can use that to our advantage. I don't just mean in relation to work either. I also mean in relation to their personal life. View your counterparty not just as an employee of their company but as a whole person.

For example, what if promotion is a real key driver for the person you are negotiating with? What if you have been able to establish that, if they could get the deal with you here today, their chances of promotion might be increased? If you know this, you might be able to use it. Similarly, if you know that your counterparty is a new parent, then you might be able to build rapport by sharing stories of sleepless nights, and this could influence how the rest of the negotiation then unfolds.

The advice here is not to get too bogged down in what

matters to you. Of course, it's important to be clear in your own mind about what success and failure looks like to you and what all the different elements of the deal are to you. The trick is to make sure you know it for them as well.

The second real danger associated with not getting inside their head is that not only might you miss an opportunity, but you might also really anger them. You see, a mistake that many people will make at the negotiation table is to assume that their priorities are matched by their counterparty's priorities. They approach the negotiation thinking that everyone around the table wants the same things or values them to the same degree. The reality, however, is that different people value and interpret things differently; your priorities might not be their priorities. Why is this an issue? Because people don't like to feel that you haven't taken them seriously, listened to them or considered their point of view.

One of the things that my team sees on our workshops is people approaching negotiations assuming that each side wants the same thing or that everyone prioritises the same issue. Just because you prioritise securing a certain level of fee and a defined delivery date doesn't mean that the other party will also prioritise these things. They might be more concerned with quality assurance or credit terms. Don't assume. You have to take the time to really uncover what matters to them. By doing this, you can start to frame your proposals in such a way that it becomes clear that you have at least started to understand their issues, and, as a result, they will feel far more valued and listened to.

Of course, there will always be variables in which both parties have an interest. This is inevitable, and these are often the areas that are the most difficult to negotiate an agreement on, as you are likely to have conflicting views. As a good example, price will often be a key driver for each side in assessing their success in a negotiation. Often, the buyer will want to pay the lowest price possible, and the seller will want to secure the highest price possible. In these situations where each side will be approaching a key issue with very different aims, you can use your understanding of all of the other issues that they might prioritise to try to craft a deal that not only works for you but works for them too. For instance, as the seller, you might be able to convince the buyer to pay a higher price if you incentivise them with another of their priorities, such as deferred payment. Developing and using a knowledge of their priorities can be an effective way to smooth over any potential areas of conflict.

There is a third danger in not fully understanding your counterparty, which is that you may be giving them the emotional upper hand. Have you ever been in a negotiation with someone who is really intimidating? Someone who is incredibly assertive, outspoken, confident and completely unflappable? Nothing you do or say seems to sway them at all. You begin to dread having to engage with them. They make you question your own ability. They are your negotiation nemesis. Getting inside their head is the first step to bringing the balance of power back over to you. Because that confident, intimidating, unflappable person is only human too. If you could get inside their head, you would see that they also have pressures, priorities, a boss, deadlines, fears, ambitions, a conditional bonus, a mortgage to pay, family and aspirations. All of those things will be whirling around inside their head during a negotiation. The more you know about what those things are, the stronger your position will be, and the stronger you will start to feel.

In Part Three, we'll come back to the psychology of negotiation, working on negotiating with different people and how to bring back the balance of power with different counterparties.

Mistake Ten: Uncertainty on making the first move

Whenever I or my team run a negotiation workshop, regardless of where it is in the world, or the industry in which we are running it, we will always ask delegates the same question: 'Who should make the first move?' Interestingly, this is often one of the most controversial issues in the workshop; it causes more questioning and pushback than anything else we teach on our sessions.

So, who should go first? In eight out of ten cases, the answer we get back from people in the room is 'the other side'. This response is pretty standard, regardless of experience, seniority, geography, industry or culture. I have also watched hundreds of negotiation role plays and case studies and seen many examples in which people desperately try to avoid making their offer first. They will often say something like this:

'You go first.'
'No! I asked you; you tell me.'
'I'll tell you once you've told me.'
'Well, I'd rather not say.'
'No, give me your number first.'

These are all classic examples of the kind of avoidance tactics we see once it gets to the stage when someone has to make the first move. There has certainly been misguided 'wisdom' spread around that you should always try to get the other side to go first. In fact, a great many 'sales skills' workshops advocate this method.

However, making the first offer in negotiation is one of the best understood and most compelling tactics to help you end up with a deal that is preferable to you. The volume and quality of research on this point is huge, and I would challenge you to find any robust evidence or research that points to the contrary.

The very simple reason why going first in a negotiation can be so powerful is because of something called **anchoring**. Anchoring is the cognitive bias that sees even the smartest of people being too heavily influenced by the information that is put first on the table. This might be in relation to the price of a product or service, the terms of a contract or a salary increase. By making the first move in a negotiation, you are essentially anchoring the other party to your starting point because right there and then, it is the focus of everyone's attention. This can then lead the other party to shift their expectations about at they can get from the deal, and can lead to you walking away with a more favourable outcome.

The research findings on making the first move in a negotiation and the power of anchoring are numerous. Headline findings include:

- If you go first you are far more likely to walk away with the preferential result.[3]

- Anchoring still impacts your counterparty even when they are an expert and should know better.[4]

- It happens even when we are warned that it might impact our response.

Put simply, you should make the first move, as that way you have more of a chance to grab and maintain the advantage. Yet we continuously look to the other party to get the ball rolling and go first. Why does this cause us such problems? Why are we so unwilling to put our offer on the table and make the first move? More often than not, it comes down to uncertainty, lack of confidence and insufficient preparation. Here are a couple of common reasons I hear for not wanting to make the first move, and tips to help you move past them.

1. But I want to know what they are willing to give me.
Negotiation is not about waiting to hear what they are prepared to give and then responding. It is about developing and presenting proposals and packages in such a way that you get them to agree to what you want. By waiting

for them to set the boundaries as to what the agreement is going to look like, you are walking into the trap of agreeing to a deal that is designed from their perspective – it's going to work in their favour, not yours! Do not wait to hear what they are willing to give you. Instead, do your research (see the next point) and let them know what *you* might be willing to give *them*.

2. What if I go first and I get my opening figure totally wrong?

People are often concerned that their opening position might be so inappropriate that they end up agreeing a deal far below what they could have got or annoying the other party so much that they end up deadlocking or coming to blows. If you have effectively explored the product, service or market in question, researched your counterparty and their situation, and are clear on your own value, worth and position, then you should be able to craft an opening proposal that is both ambitious and realistic. Take a look at Mistake Eleven for more on this point.

So what happens if you don't get to go first?

Of course, there are always going to be situations where you can't go first. Maybe in your industry there are regulations and norms which require that one side makes the first proposal, or maybe you just don't get in there quickly enough. Make sure you don't fall into the following traps.

Don't keep going on about it!

A common trap that people fall into is to keep going on and on about the proposal which has just been made to them. They respond with incredulity or disbelief and begin to critically analyse the detail of what has been suggested. It's not uncommon for people to just keep repeating back the proposal they have just heard, almost as if they were mimicking their counterparty:

> *'How much? £4,000? Really? £4,000 is ridiculous for this. Seriously, if you think £4,000 is a price I can accept, then you are sorely mistaken. £4,000? Come on!'*

After all your shock, disbelief and 'rejection' of their £4,000 proposal, what have you achieved? Nothing. You've not gone anywhere, you've not moved from the £4,000; instead you are still right there, anchored to that £4,000.

I view that initial £4,000 proposal as a deflated balloon. At the point when it's put out onto the negotiation table, it is pretty empty. It's very much present and is the only thing we all have to look at, but it could be made bigger by blowing into it. Which is exactly what you do every time you talk about that £4,000 balloon, and it gets bigger and bigger and bigger.

Don't ask them to explain themselves

The next thing people will do is ask their counterparty to explain the proposal they just made. You might think that this is a sensible thing to do: that by asking them to explain themselves they will somehow see the error of their ways, fall over their own point of view and end up undermining themselves.

This very rarely happens. In most situations, by the time people get to the negotiation table they have already invested a lot of time, energy and enthusiasm 'buying into' their own position. Of course they will be able to explain themselves, and probably very eloquently too. All the while, they are blowing into that £4,000 balloon.

We also need to think about the purpose of asking for their explanation. If you have just been presented with a proposal that you could never agree to or accept, why bother asking them to explain themselves? All you have done is waste valuable time listening to an explanation that makes absolutely no difference as to whether or not you can agree. And you have reinforced and strengthened their anchor. So, if you know you can't agree to it, don't waste valuable time asking them to explain it to you. There are far better ways of getting what you want.

Don't be swayed by it

One of the worst things you can do if the other party goes first is to allow it to cloud your judgement. Imagine that your counterparty is the buyer and they go first and offer you far less than you had anticipated they would for your product or service. The danger is that you then reposition your request to look more 'reasonable' or in line with the one they have just made. This can be the case even when you have done your research and are confident on your opening position.

Dragged down by an anchor

Imagine that you are looking to sell your shirt, and I am looking buy it from you. You might be thinking to yourself that you are going to ask for £20, and that you would be happy to settle for slightly less than that. However, before you can open your mouth to say anything, I jump in and say: 'I like that shirt. I am prepared to offer you £6 for it.'

The mistake people often make is that they then deviate from their plan. When I make my very low proposal to you, the little voice in your head might start to say to you: '£6? That's way lower than I thought she would offer. Maybe I was being a bit overambitious with £20 ... Maybe I should ask for less, or else I might look a bit greedy.' Then when you do open your mouth to make your proposal, you say: 'Sorry, I can't agree to £6. I was looking for £14.' Immediately, by moving from £20 to £14 to more closely match my proposal of £6, you have limited what you might have achieved. I might have been willing to go far, far higher than £6, but now you have ensured that I will never go higher than £14 and have vastly increased the likelihood of finishing closer to a figure that works better for me than for you.

Cast out a new anchor

So, what should you do in response to the other party going first? The best way to deal with it is to recognise that by dwelling on their proposal you are making it stronger. Instead, thank them for their proposal and then offer up your own. This way you begin to anchor what you want, from your perspective.

> *'Thanks for your proposal. However, my proposal to you is in fact ...'*

The more you get them to talk about and focus on that, the more likely you are to get it. Talk about your numbers, your position and your request.

Anchoring is real

Researchers have observed that many people struggle with the notion of anchoring and going first because it suggests a lack of free will on our part.[5] If this is you, get over it. Anchoring is real. And it matters to all of us.

So, try to go first if you can. But if you can't, for whatever reason, don't be naïve or unaware as to the impact that their opening proposal could have on you and your performance in the subsequent negotiation. Be aware. Don't fall into the trap of reinforcing or giving way to their anchor.

The exception to the rule?

I would actively encourage the other party to go first if I had just been presented, at the last minute, with a negotiation that I knew nothing about, and had no immediate way of finding anything out about before I was due to meet them. Then, along with observations about their body language, style and the words they used, I would use their first proposal as the start of my evidence to help me understand their thinking and a possible strategy.

Mistake Eleven: Not opening ambitiously enough

One of the areas that prompts some of the strongest reactions whenever we mention it, anywhere in the world, is also one of the most commonly practised tactics in negotiation. I am referring to 'opening ambitiously': the idea that the more you ask for, the more you get. I also like to refer to this as 'testing the water' or leaving yourself plenty of 'wriggle room' to explore possibilities.

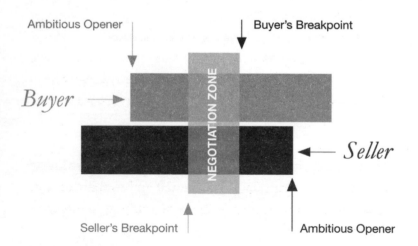

This diagram shows a basic example of how opening iously works in practice. In the housing market, it is not uncommon for a seller to place their house on the market at one level, even though they know that they will accept a slightly lower level. The first level is the seller's ambitious opener. At the same time, a buyer will initially offer a far lower amount than they know they can reach to; this is the buyer's ambitious opener. The breakpoint here is the absolute maximum the buyer can go to, and minimum the seller can go to. We'll discuss breakpoints in more detail from page 116.

The concept of asking for more than you need or offering less than you can afford really troubles some people. They find it uncomfortable, misleading and disingenuous. I will often have pushback from people saying, 'this doesn't happen in my industry', or:

> *'My clients and I are honest with each other. We don't play this game.'*
> *'Really?'* I ask. *'And how do you know that?'*
> *'I just do,'* they say.
> *'How?'* I ask. *'How do you know they are not inflating their prices ever so slightly to get that bit more out of the deal?'*

That's where it tends to go quiet. You don't always know whether the other party has opened ambitiously or not, because they are highly unlikely to tell you in advance that this is what they are doing.

> *'Hi! Just before we begin I wanted to let you know up front that I am going to start at £600, but I can*

really drop down to £520. Just letting you know in advance. Keep pushing me and I'll get to the real price eventually.'

The reality is that most people will try to explore what the best deal is that they can get, and some will do it subtly with opening proposals that aren't outlandish or ridiculous. Think of these examples:

- The seller who initially says they cannot under any circumstances accept less than £450 for their product but who ends up settling for £375.

- The buyer who says they absolutely have to have the project completed in three weeks, but they end up agreeing to four.

- The solicitor who starts by demanding £10,000 on behalf of their client and ends up settling for £7,800.

- The newly engaged couple who insist to their family that they are absolutely only having a small wedding, who end up with masses of guests who they haven't seen in years.

In all of these circumstances, the negotiator has tried to improve the chances of what they end up with by opening ambitiously. The logic is that by opening far higher or far lower than what you actually need or expect, you leave yourself room to manoeuvre, are able to explore just what the other side's boundaries might be, can make them feel like they have 'won', and can end up influencing your counterparty in such a way that they reassess what they might have been willing to agree to – either consciously or subconsciously.

Why does opening ambitiously work?

Why does this work? We're back to anchoring again. The science of anchoring isn't just about who goes first, it's also about what we choose to put out there, to what level, and the impact which that has on the end result of the negotiation. There is a stack of writing out there on opening ambitiously, but one of the most compelling examples is a piece of research conducted by Chapman and Bornstein on awards made by juries.[6]

The more you ask for, the more you get

In 1996, psychologists Gretchen Chapman and Brian Bornstein presented 80 students with identical hypothetical medical negligence cases. The students were broken up into four groups of twenty, and each of the four groups was presented with a different demand for damages from the claimant's legal team. The average award given by each 'jury member' in each group is below:

Demand	Average award
$100	$990
$20,000	$36,000
$5 million	$440,000
$1 billion	$490,000

It seems that the jurors were incredibly persuadable and guided by the 'anchoring effect' of the differing demands made by the claimant's legal team, as factually there were no other differences in the cases presented to the four groups. What is also interesting is that the seemingly 'outlandish' claim of $1 billion still resulted in a higher average award than any of the others.

The evidence shows that the more ambitious you are, and the more you ask for, the more you are likely to get. Whether we like it or not, we are influenced by the size of number that is presented to us early on in an interaction, be that an informal conversation or a more formal commercial negotiation.

When someone presents us with their number (or anchor), our brains cannot help but to think about that number. The challenge, of course, is to move away from their number as quickly as you can and start to think about an alternative that works better for you.

Amos Tversky (one of the researchers behind the famous United Nations experiment on anchoring, in which participants were asked to estimate how many African countries were part of the United Nations after spinning a wheel of fortune)[7], had a theory that anchoring is so powerful because when we are presented with the other side's anchor, we then mentally adjust it upward or downward. We will continue adjusting until we reach a zone of plausibility. And then we stop.

Tversky believed that the issue we have with moving away from ambitious openers or anchors from our counterparty is that we stop too soon. Instead of moving away from their anchor to the furthest possible point that would represent the best deal for us, we stop too readily at the first plausible, comfortable answer. Their anchor can therefore curtail our belief or ambition as to what could be achieved. And so we then make a counter-offer nothing like the one we had originally planned and are instead heavily influenced by what they have just requested of us, or anchored us to.

Opening ambitiously creates wriggle room

Refer back to page 65 on the impact of an ambitious first move on our perception of what the possible boundaries of the deal might be. But understanding the effect on you only works if you then go on to *move*. One of my mantras is that negotiation is all about movement. The point being that if each side refuses to move, then you actually have a stand-off, not a negotiation. This is particularly true when it comes to opening ambitiously. If you open ambitiously but then refuse to move from that potentially extreme point, you are cancelling out the benefit that movement can bring.

Opening ambitiously can have the bizarre effect of making your counterparty feel like they are winning. Let's imagine you and I are negotiating. The company I work for sells a service that you would like to buy. Because I understand the benefits of opening ambitiously and anchoring, I make the first offer of £17,500 for my company's services, even though I know I could go as low as £15,000 (my breakpoint).

You had been anticipating spending far less than this and respond with: 'OK, that's a lot more than we had budgeted for. I was thinking closer to £14,500.' At this point, the balance of power sits firmly with me, as I am then able to make use of my wriggle room (having started at £17,500). I respond with: 'OK. I can't go that low, but if you can pay us in 20 days rather than 30, then I can drop to £16,220.'

And right then, at that moment, you have won. You have managed to secure a drop on the price from me, I have moved towards you and therefore, psychologically, you have scored a victory. Of course, so have I, as not only have I secured £1,220 more than my breakpoint, I have also secured more preferential standard payment terms. I have immediately cast myself as the person who is willing to be creative and flexible when it comes to trying to reach a deal, and you are happy because you have moved me from my opening proposal. A 2002 study supports this assertion: researchers discovered that negotiators were much more dissatisfied when a first offer was accepted than they were with achieving the same outcome after multiple rounds of negotiating.[8]

The thing is, you can only move in the way I have in this example if you open ambitiously in the first place. Let's instead imagine that I believe opening ambitiously is in some way disingenuous or unethical. So, I decide that transparency is the best option to progress the relationship and get a deal done. This time I make a commitment to share my actual breakpoint of £15,000. This is how I open:

'Great to see you. Look, I don't want to waste your time, so I can tell you straight away that my best price is going to be £15,000. I hope you appreciate that I'm being honest with you on this, as I really value our relationship.'

'OK. I'm really going to need something closer to £14,500,' you reply. *'Can you make any move on that?'*

'Sorry! No can do. £15,000 really is the best I can manage. I really was being honest that I can't do better on price.'

'So you're saying that you are not prepared to move at all? Is there nothing you can do?

'I really can't shift on that price. I'm trying to do the right thing here.'

'Really? It feels to me like you're just digging your heels in. This doesn't feel much like a partnership to me.'

At this point I have two options. I can choose to stay where I am, sticking at my 'honest and transparent' opening proposal with a frustrated counterparty, or I can move. The problem is that because I didn't open ambitiously and went straight in with my breakpoint, if I do move closer to £14,500, then I start to lose in terms of the overall value of the deal. My profit margin risks being eroded, dangerous precedents are set, and neither side feels satisfied with the deal because the whole interaction has felt like a battle.

When is ambitious *too* ambitious?

While opening ambitiously is essential, it is always worth being mindful of the point at which you have opened too ambitiously, the point at which the proposal lacks any form of credibility and becomes ridiculous. We call this the Get Real Point. It's the point at which your counter-party might well tell you to 'get real', and you run the risk of damaging both your credibility and the deal.

So, how ambitious is too ambitious? There is no magic formula. The barrier really depends on a number of different factors and can change from negotiation to negotiation. It might be impacted by a previous relationship, the people present in the room, past conversations, the industry in which you operate, precedents, legislation, etc. Consideration of all of these factors and what might constitute the walk-away barrier should be a key part of your negotiation planning.

However, experience has taught me that the worry is seldom whether you have been too ambitious; it's more frequently the case that people are not ambitious enough. You'll know instantly if they accept your 'ambitious opener' straight away with no questions asked that you have completely misjudged the issues and boundaries in this deal. If they accept your opening offer happily, you haven't been ambitious enough. I always advise my clients to work out their ambitious opener and then add on another 10 per cent, just to counter the tendency most of us have to misjudge what we really mean by 'ambitious'!

Because of the power of anchoring, the next time you get to the negotiation table you need to:

- Go first if you can – but know how to deal with it if you don't.

- When you do make a proposal, open ambitiously, but credibly.

Mistake Twelve: Arguing rather than negotiating

You will never win an argument in a negotiation. Ever. A lot of people confuse the act of arguing with the act of negotiating. They think that being an amazing negotiator is all about their ability to effectively contradict or undermine the position of their counterparty.

There is no denying that the ability to formulate your point of view in a persuasive way will help you in the wider negotiation process. But that's not what we're looking at here. We're talking about a full-on, heated argument or relentless bickering over the details – something I see happening way too frequently with negotiators of all levels of experience. The mistaken assumption is that arguing will you bring some kind of benefit. However, often it merely wastes time and limits the potential outcome at the negotiation table.

Imagine that you are sitting down to negotiate. Your counterparty makes a proposal of £12,500 for your product. You are visibly unhappy with this and respond argumentatively by saying:

'How much? Really? Are you joking? That is an absolutely ridiculous proposal, which leads me to believe that you can't have done your research

properly. Did you just pluck that figure out of thin air?
My product is worth much more than that.'

How likely is it that your counterparty will respond
like this?

'You know what? You're right. That is a ridiculous
proposal. I really didn't do as much research as I
should have done. I'm sure your product is worth a lot
more. I'm so embarrassed. Pretend I never said it, and
let's just go with whatever you want.'

Very unlikely indeed. And why is that? Because when
someone tries to argue with us and contradict our position, nine times out of ten we will dig down and defend
it. And that's when the argument escalates, tempers get
frayed, the atmosphere grows tense and each side tries a
number of different methods to show that they are right
and the other side is wrong.

At the end of the negotiation you might well limp your
way to a deal, and you might think you've got one over on
your counterparty, but is that going to be the best, most
creative, innovative and value-focused deal you could
have got? Or is it one based on annoyance, resentment
and frustration? Your counterparty likes you far less
than they did before, which certainly won't work in your
favour if you ever have to see or work with them again.

Instead of falling into the trap of bickering, learn to
recognise that the best way to beat their proposal is not
to argue with them over it. Simply move away from it.

Defuse it by suggesting an alternative. Repackage the proposal in a different way. Suggest that you agree to disagree and look for an alternative together. Call a time out and let everyone cool down. Just don't think that arguing with them is ever going to be a good use of time. Resist the urge and move things on.

Mistake Thirteen: Fearing 'no' – when 'no' is just a springboard to 'maybe'

Nobody really likes to hear the word 'no'. Rejection is something that doesn't sit well with most people. We learn from a young age that 'no' means that we can't get what we want, that we have been restricted or chastised, or that what we wanted is in some way negative or simply unattainable to us.

We have a neurological oversensitivity to the word 'no'.[9] Our brains will hang on to the hurt associated with a rejection or a 'no' for far longer than they will the happiness of a victory or a 'yes'.

It's certainly true that in negotiation many people hear the word 'no' and crumble. They lose focus. They feel frustrated or embarrassed. They retreat from the issue they were proposing or discussing and flounder around trying to come up with some kind of alternative. Failing that, they go quiet. They end up taking a back seat and allowing the other side to take the lead.

The problem is that in a negotiation you are going to have to hear the word 'no'. It is highly likely that you are going to experience some form of rejection. So, we need to protect ourselves from the pain and discomfort of hearing 'no'. We can't just fall apart every time someone disagrees with our proposal. We need to retrain our brain and redefine our relationship with 'no': take ownership of it and turn it on its head.

The way that we do this is to start to view 'no' differently. Don't see it as the end! Instead, see it as the beginning. Use the 'no' as a cue to explore with your counterparty what could be possible. Acknowledge their 'no'. Ask questions. Gather insight. Propose alternatives. Use 'what if' to explore potential scenarios with them. See 'no' as your springboard to all the other potential options out there. A good negotiator is curious, so use the 'no' as your permission to be just that.

Start to nudge that 'no' towards being a 'maybe', and then all you have to do is nudge that 'maybe' to a 'yes'. 'No' is simply the springboard to 'maybe' and all that lies after it. As Frank Underwood, the ruthless politician in the TV show *House of Cards*, says: 'You can't turn a "no" into a "yes" without a "maybe" in between.'

Mistake Fourteen: Always trying to be 'fair'

I don't know many people who wouldn't like to be described as fair. Fair is good. Governments talk of creating a fair society; union representatives talk about fair pay; sporting bodies talk about fair play; international agencies talk about fair trade. The notion that something is fair makes the topic it has been partnered with immediately more appealing to most people. We can relate to it. We feel comfortable with it. Fairness is balanced, ethical, impartial and just.

But it's also subjective. And herein lies the problem. You see, during the negotiation process, many people will use fairness as their guide. They will develop proposals that seem fair to each side. But there are some real problems with allowing fairness to be the yardstick for your negotiations.

While in each society there is a commonly held set of principles as to what constitutes fairness (based loosely on ideas of being balanced, ethical, impartial and just), individuals in different situations will view fairness differently. For example, a buyer might make a proposal which seems very fair to them based on the market research they have done. However, to the seller that proposal might seem anything but, based on their experience – all the costs and hard work – of what has gone into creating, marketing and selling the product. What a teenager views as fair might not be a view shared by their parents. What seems fair to a commuter struggling to get to work during a transport strike might not be what is viewed as fair by those workers who have instigated the strike. What might seem fair to a group of squatters who have taken residence of an empty home will most likely not be seen as fair by the young family living next door, who have been saving for years to afford a mortgage on their home, on what had been a quiet residential street.

People will interpret things differently depending on the angle from which they are viewing the problem or issue. This is a phenomenon that is well understood in the practice of mediation.

Don't forget that the notion of fairness is also quite

variable in different parts of the world. In the UK, the notion of fairness can be viewed as providing additional support to those in a weaker position than most, whereas in Japanese society, fairness is viewed as treating all people exactly the same, irrespective of their differences and situation.

Be careful of 'selling your fairness'

You should be very cautious of trying to 'sell your fairness' to your counterparty during a negotiation, especially if you think that they might be coming at it from a very different perspective to you.

An illustration of this in practice would be one side in the negotiation making their proposal to the other side and ending their suggestion with: '... and I think that's a very fair proposal, don't you?' They shouldn't be surprised to hear a reaction along the lines of: 'Er, no actually. That doesn't feel very fair at all. It might be to you but it certainly isn't for me.'

Attempting to 'sell' your fairness to your counterparty can result in them growing irritated with you and lashing out at your misguided assessment of what constitutes 'fair'. So, avoid using fairness as the justification for your proposal; if they are on the opposite side of the negotiation, it's highly likely that their interpretation of fairness differs slightly to yours.

Finally, remember that not everyone will be pleased if fairness is your guide, even if they agree with your definition – especially in the workplace. What might happen if you allowed fairness to shape every decision you made at the negotiating table? Imagine you are negotiating with a supplier and you decide to pay them an extra 10 per cent above the standard price for their product, as you think that would be the fair thing to do. Now try explaining that one to your boss. Or to the Board. Or to the shareholders. Your explanation that it 'felt like the fair thing to do' isn't really going to fly. I imagine at this point you would be desperately hoping that your firm had a really 'fair' severance policy.

Mistake Fifteen: Obsessing about getting to 'yes'

Of course I am being tongue in cheek here! Many of you will have read the fantastic negotiation book *Getting to Yes* by Fisher and Ury. *Getting to Yes* is considered by many to be the blueprint for collaborative deal-making and for understanding the concept of win/win and principled negotiation. It has shaped and influenced millions of negotiators (myself included) since it was published in 1981. Common Negotiation Mistake Fifteen is certainly not a criticism of *Getting to Yes*.

What I am actually referring to is our obsession with hearing the word 'yes' at the negotiation table (the direct opposite of Mistake Thirteen: fearing the word 'no'). In simple terms, we view 'yes' as success. We want to hear it said to us and ideally as soon as possible. In the same way that there are negative connotations with the word 'no', the reverse (unsurprisingly) is true when it comes to the word 'yes'. We like hearing 'yes'. It makes us feel happy. It makes us feel successful and like we have achieved something. Because if they say 'yes', then surely we must have then achieved what we really wanted, right? Well, not necessarily.

What if it comes way too easily? Should we then still view 'yes' as a success? I believe we should be extremely cautious of the 'yes' that comes too easily or is handed to us on a plate. If our counterparty says 'yes' to our first proposal, we shouldn't view that as cause for celebration. It should instead be a big red warning flag that we have misunderstood the potential boundaries of the negotiation. It probably means we didn't open ambitiously enough. An immediate 'yes' means that accepting our proposal was easy for them. It means we have probably got nothing like the best deal they could have given us. An immediate 'yes' means we haven't fully explored what might have been possible.

In our quest to get to 'yes' we often overlook the fact that negotiation is about exploration, examining possibilities and looking at ways to maximise outcomes. As part of this process we should expect to hear a 'no' or a 'maybe'.

Sometimes a 'yes' just isn't worth having

We should also remember that sometimes the best deal we do is the one we walk away from. Sometimes, even after all your best efforts, the deal that's being offered to you by the other side just isn't what you had planned for. If you agree to the deal, you might find that you are hurting yourself or your company, as it just doesn't represent a positive outcome, a sustainable solution to a problem or value for money.

The problem is that a lot of people view deadlock or an inability to reach an agreement that works for both sides as a failure on their part. *Surely all brilliant negotiators should be able to turn it around and get a great result?* Well, no. Not always. There will always be occasions where the numbers just don't add up, the logistics won't work out or the differences of opinion can't be reconciled, no matter what you do.

In those situations, it doesn't make you a poor negotiator if you walk away from the deal. It makes you a poor negotiator if you go ahead with the deal because you are so focused on getting that 'yes', even if you know deep down that the agreement doesn't make sense.

Mistake Sixteen: Making empty threats and pointless ultimatums

There is something very powerful in an ultimatum, isn't there? It lets people know you mean business and can really focus the mind. That said, this is only true if the ultimatum is a genuine and credible one.

There are certain phrases used by negotiators that always grab my attention, mostly because I'm keen to see if what they are saying is true or whether they are making empty threats and pointless ultimatums.

My best/final price is …
I really can't go any lower than …
Under no circumstance will I accept …
… and that really is my maximum.

My final, final, final price

One member of my advantageSPRING training team had been sent to run a negotiation workshop for a group of experienced lawyers in the City of London. During a role-play exercise, one of the more senior partners in the room made a proposal to their allotted counterparty: 'OK, £7,000. That's my final offer.' Of course, based on the case study, my colleague knew that it certainly wasn't the final offer they could make, so they waited to see how the delegate would position their subsequent moves. It went something like this:

> 'That's not something I can accept. My final, final offer is £8,100.'
>
> 'I could move to £8,600, but that really is my maximum.'
>
> 'I see. That's not going to work for me. My final, final, final offer is £9,000. Take it or leave it.'

And they did a deal at £10,200. At what point did the senior partner lose their credibility? Simple. It was the second they said that something was their final offer and then moved from it.

The point is that when used correctly, these types of phrases can send a very powerful message to your counterparty that they need to listen up, take you seriously and make a proposal based on your stated requirement.

Where these phrases lose all their power and start to eat away at your credibility is when you use them and then immediately contradict yourself. By stating that something is your final offer and then immediately conceding on that point, you send the message that your word means nothing. People start to take you less seriously than they did before.

I'm not saying that you should stop using those phrases; just don't fall into the trap of using them inappropriately. The test for what defines inappropriate use is a simple two steps:

- If the ultimatum isn't actually true and you could make more moves: only use it as part of a defined strategy to elicit further concessions from them or to allow you to walk away and 'reconsider' (at least for a time).

- If the ultimatum is true and it *really* is your final offer: use it.

If you are selective about using these phrases and you don't overuse them, when you do say them, people will know you really mean business.

Mistake Seventeen: Assuming that good things come to those who wait

Last year I spoke at a business networking event in London about some of the common mistakes made by negotiators. As part of the session, I encouraged people to ask for what they want. To stand up. To negotiate.

A woman in the audience put up her hand and said: 'I think you are being flippant. If you are that person who is always asking for more, always trying to haggle or always speaking up, then you will be perceived negatively.' She went on to say: 'At some point, you just have to accept that good things will come to good people and if you work hard, you will be rewarded.'[10]

A stunned silence fell on the room as I and most of the rest of the audience thought about what she had said. Then one of the other members of the audience piped up with: 'Come on! Get real!' I'm afraid have to agree. Get real.

In an ideal world, maybe this would be the case. Maybe we would all automatically be recognised and rewarded for our achievements. Maybe we wouldn't have to ask for what we want. But that's not the world we live in right now. We live in a world where fortune favours the bold. Rather than passively waiting for someone to recognise our achievements or needs, we should speak up. We would be foolish to assume that our boss, partner, counterparty or colleague could read our minds. If we want something, we need to be able to ask for it. To be able to initiate the difficult conversation. To tell people what we want. We just need to do it in the right way (which Part Three of this book is all about!).

So, instead of taking a chance on karma and waiting for good things to come to you, take a chance on yourself. To be a great negotiator you need to be in charge, know what you want and, most importantly, make sure you ask.

Mistake Eighteen: Thinking you are a special case

A common misconception is that negotiation differs from industry to industry. I regularly meet people who insist that many of the points we teach just would not apply to them in the job that they do. The fact is that your industry is not unique when it comes to negotiation. As a principle and a process, negotiation is pretty much universal.

Whether you are buying a house, selling advertising space, agreeing terms of an employment contract, debating a rota for household chores, allocating workload among a team, disputing a legal claim or negotiating terms of an international trade agreement, the same kinds of principles will apply. Each side is likely to have their own issues and priorities, each side is likely to have aspirations, and each side is likely to have identified a breakpoint or bottom line. In all these examples, there will need to be a process of constructing a deal (often many times over) and then closing the deal. All will be influenced by the people involved, and there will be different tactics used at different times to try to influence the outcome.

What might well change from negotiation to negotiation are the issues. For example, the issues being negotiated in a house sale might be price, availability date and an extension to the leasehold. The issues being negotiated in an international trade agreement might be volume, price, signatories, movement of goods and local taxation.

The point is that there are certain principles in negotiation which exist no matter what the negotiation is. Once we learn these principles, we can apply them to different negotiations, at different times and in different ways. Whether you are a buyer or seller, claimant or defendant, working in law, construction, finance or retail, it will be of huge benefit to you to learn these principles. It's then up to you to learn the specific nuances, rules, norms and regulations that apply to the specific industry or negotiation you are in.

Mistake Nineteen: Assuming that everyone shares your values

If I were to show you the two boxes of behaviours below and ask you which set you would rather be on the receiving end of, which set you would rather exhibit to others, or which set makes you feel more comfortable, which would you choose?

Box A	Box B
Generous	Unreasonable
Rational	Rejecting
Truthful	Arrogant
Considerate	Untruthful
Dependable	Closed
Reasonable	Inconsiderate
Cooperative	Selfish

Unsurprisingly, most people will choose Box A. The simple reason for this is that Box A is very positive. It includes behaviours that we are encouraged to exhibit from a very young age. They are behaviours that we would like our boss to use to describe us in a performance review; they are behaviours we would look for in a potential partner or in our friends; and they are the words I would like to see being used in my little boy's school report. In short, these are words that reassure us. They are comforting and make us feel upbeat and optimistic.

Box B presents another story altogether. The list of behaviours in Box B is not particularly positive. These are not behaviours we are encouraged to show from a young age. These are not the words you would like to see in your performance review, that you look for in your friends or future partner, and if I saw those words being used in my son's school report I would immediately be on the phone trying to book an urgent appointment with his teacher to discuss just what exactly is going wrong. These words do not reassure us. They generally make us feel uncomfortable and cause us stress and discomfort.

Why does this matter?

We would almost always rather be in a situation that involves us receiving and using Box A behaviours than we would Box B behaviours. And yet, Box B behaviours are the ones that are routinely used by negotiators.

Let's be clear on a few points. First, I'm not saying that in order to be an amazing negotiator you should use all of the Box B behaviours at once. If you came to negotiate with me and started chucking out all of the Box B behaviours, I would think you were a ridiculous comedy villain, and I just wouldn't take you seriously. Second, I'm not saying that the aim of this book is to teach you how to be arrogant, unreasonable and selfish!

What I am saying is that sometimes when you negotiate, you might have to exhibit some of those Box B behaviours. You might not like it or feel comfortable with it, but the situation might well call for it. (Remember Mistake Seven: Trying to get too comfortable?)

Box B behaviours in practice

During a negotiation you might not be able to reveal every scrap of information you have to your counterparty. This might be for legal, ethical, data protection, confidentiality or operational issues. As a result of this you are going to have to be **closed**.

Similarly, if your counterparty keeps asking for something that you simply cannot, under any circumstances, concede to, you are going to have to be **rejecting**. And as a result, they might perceive you for a time as **unreasonable**.

The point is that we might not like doing it, but sometimes we are going to have to behave in ways during a negotiation that don't come naturally to us. Our job is to find a way to do it credibly and confidently and with the minimum of nerves. More importantly though, we need to recognise that some people don't struggle with these behaviours at all. They either come quite naturally to them, or they have taken the time to practise them so that they can turn them on and off when they most need to. People will sometimes choose to exhibit Box B behaviours because they know that they will make you feel uncomfortable – and that this discomfort might have an effect on your performance at the negotiation table.

Are you telling me I have to lie?

When I talk to people about the Box B behaviours, someone will inevitably say: 'You have used the word 'untruthful'! Are you saying I have to lie to be a brilliant negotiator?'

My answer to this question is unequivocal: no. I am not saying you have to lie to be a brilliant negotiator. I know that for many people the notion of lying is abhorrent. For many people it is a line they will not cross. They worry that lying in business is unethical and potentially illegal. For a lot of people, whether or not they lie is non-negotiable. You know what? That's fine.

What's not fine is automatically assuming that your counterparty shares your values, which includes your attitude towards lying. The danger is that, in assuming your counterparty has also chosen not to lie, you don't question or doubt anything they tell you in the negotiation.

Experience tells me that lying is subjective. You might think it's a very black-and-white area, but people's views on lying are rarely as simple as for or against. There are many shades of grey.

- Some people view withholding little bits of commercial information as an intelligent strategy. Others view it as deceptive, underhand and untruthful.

- Some people are happy to tell 'little white lies' or 'bend the truth' if it gets a result. Others view that as disingenuous or unethical.

- Some people will tell a huge, barefaced lie and view it as 'simply business'. Others view it as wholly unacceptable and (potentially) illegal.

They don't tell you upfront

Many of our workshop delegates will insist to us that they are 100 per cent certain that their counterparty is being open and transparent with them, that as trusted partners they wouldn't engage in deceit to get a better outcome.

The thing is, it's not always easy to tell if someone is lying to you at the negotiation table. Sure, you can read their body language and look for signals in the words they use, but that's not always foolproof ... or easy.

For me, the bigger issue is that you can't always know if someone is lying to you because they are highly unlikely to tell you upfront that this is what they are doing (just as is the case with opening ambitiously). I don't know anyone who starts a negotiation with the line: 'Just so you know, everything I say for the first ten minutes or so is not true ... just telling you upfront. Keep pushing me and I'll get to the real numbers eventually'. It's up to you to insulate yourself and your deal.

Get cynical

So, how do we deal with lying? The simple answer is to get cynical. Don't automatically assume that the other side is always telling you the whole truth just because that is a boundary you have set for yourself.

At the negotiation table you have a responsibility to yourself, your client or the company you represent to try to get the best deal you can. This requires you to listen, push back, ask questions and explore the limits and deadlines they give you. Test what they are telling you so you can start to feel more confident that it's the truth. The fact is that lies will often unravel pretty quickly if challenged, explored or unpicked effectively.

To help with this, the DEALS method outlined in Part Two is designed to help you plan effectively and gather all of the information you need, so that it will be far harder for a lie to continue masquerading as the truth. In Chapter Five, we will also examine the strategies we can adopt when we are presented with obvious or proven lies during a negotiation.

Mistake Twenty: Thinking there is such a thing as a natural-born negotiator

There is no such thing as a natural-born negotiator. People who term themselves as such are often the ones who skimp on planning and preparation, understanding their counterparty and exploring possible opportunities that are not immediately obvious. In short, they are the ones who tend to get the OK deal, rather than the exceptional one.

Negotiation is a blend of a range of skills, strengths, processes and practices. It can be taught and it can be learned. Practice is key. So, now we've cleared that up, why don't you go on to read about how to do just that?

The DEALS Method

Now we have explored some of the things that we *shouldn't* be doing as negotiators, I want to provide you with some insight into what you *should* be doing to make sure that you get the best deal, every time. The chapters in Part Two provide you with tips, tools and advice to use before, during and after your negotiations.

When my team works with clients, we encourage them to understand that negotiation is as much about people as it is about process. You can't have one without the other – or if you do, you are going to end up with a substandard result compared to what you could have achieved if you had understood and embraced both. In this section we will focus mainly on process, although there are going to be elements of the 'human aspect' of negotiation woven throughout. In Part Three we will be looking at the psychology of negotiation and the impact that human behaviour has on the deals that we do.

When it comes to the process of negotiation, it's essential you get the planning and preparation right; otherwise you won't be able to perform to the fullest during the interaction. Similarly, there is no point performing brilliantly in the negotiation if you don't then conclude or 'seal' the deal in the right way so that you can follow up issues such as poor performance or changing requirements. There are no shortcuts to being a brilliant negotiator. It requires time, effort, practice, insight, information and the development of multiple options. Unfortunately, getting it wrong could have severe implications in your personal and professional life.

Many people find the process of negotiation daunting. To help people see that negotiation is something they can master, I have developed the DEALS method:

Discover
Establish
Ask
Lead
Seal

DEALS is a simple and memorable acronym that summarises the different, essential stages in the negotiation process. This section follows the DEALS approach, and provides a simple step-by-step guide to what we should be doing before, during and after we negotiate.

CHAPTER THREE

Discover

A woodsman was once asked, 'What would you do if you had just five minutes to chop down a tree?' He answered, 'I would spend the first two and a half minutes sharpening my axe.'[11]

The D of the DEALS method is all about what happens before you get anywhere near to the negotiation table. Planning and preparation is of fundamental importance to any negotiation, large or small, and is what allows you to understand the possible opportunities, possible threats, possible proposals, possible stumbling blocks and possible outcomes.

But it is often tempting to skimp on this part. We all lead busy lives. We don't have hours to spare digging around trying to find out information. Time is scarce. When coaching individuals or training teams, I will often hear:

I don't need to do all of this, do I?
Yes. You really do.

I don't have time.
Make time. Or find some help.

I've negotiated this kind of deal loads of times ...
I've seen it all before ... I can deal with whatever is
thrown at me.
'Winging it' is never a sensible negotiation
strategy. Ever.

Do not fall into the trap of thinking that the planning and preparation phase can be bypassed. It is absolutely essential to ensure you have fully understood the issues in the negotiation, as well as the priorities and concerns of both your counterparty and yourself.

This following section is designed to help you *maximise* the planning and preparation period so that you can be more effective and focused. I recognise that time is precious. So let's make sure that you use it wisely.

Know your negotiation

The first thing you need to do is to define the negotiation. You need to explore and understand all of the possible angles and outcomes that exist in this possible deal. Among other things you need to be clear on the issue, product, service or position being negotiated; who the main players are going to be; why and when this negotiation is going to take place; and what the possible influencing factors will be on this deal. We call this building your 'Insight Locker'. The following checklist can help you make sure that you have explored all of the issues that might start to influence your potential deal.

The Insight Locker checklist – who, what, when, where, why

- What are you negotiating?
- Why are you negotiating it?
- Could anything else be brought to the table?
- What 'type' of negotiation is this?
- Who is likely to be involved?
- When is it likely to take place?
- What is the history?
- Where has this come from?
- Has this been negotiated before?
- What are the associated risks? For you and them.
- Do you have an alternative? Do they have an alternative?
- What does success look like?
- What does failure look like?
- Are you missing any information?
- How do you think they are likely to behave?
- Likely time frame?
- Are there any political, economic or reputational implications for this deal?

Once you have gathered as much relevant information as you can to answer the questions in this checklist, it would be wise to reflect on exactly what type of negotiation you are in (see our discussion of the Five Factor Test in Common Negotiation Mistake Five, page 40). Is it a competitive or Value Claim negotiation, or a collaborative or Value Create negotiation? It might seem ridiculously obvious what type of negotiation you're facing, but many people will assume that it's one type, then, upon scratching the surface, they see that the reality is quite different. At this point, analyse the five defining factors, don't just make an assumption.

What effective research can protect against

A good example is the counterparty who contacts you requesting that you come together to negotiate supply of a product. They mention that they are interested in a partnership with the successful supplier and that they intend to engage them in a long-term contract which could be really lucrative and based on mutual value.

So, you prepare for the negotiation on the assumption that this is a collaborative affair with a future potential partner. You become excited at the prospect of what this could mean and start to look for ways to show them what a great partner you would be. You cut your pricing, extend your payment terms and offer them additional extras to show what great value for money you could be.

And guess what? You win the deal! You are elated. You sign the contract on incredibly beneficial terms for them, and you are optimistic about what the future partnership might deliver. But the partnership never delivers. The contracts never come. Your once effusive counterparty has suddenly gone cold.

If you had carried out research and filled your Insight Locker before this negotiation, you might have been able to establish that this company works with multiple suppliers, has a reputation for driving down hard on price, and has recently recruited a number of new buyers from a company with a history of delivering cost efficiencies. You might also have discovered that the buyer you spoke with is about to get married and is talking on social media about how he hopes his bonus will cover the cost of his exotic honeymoon ... All of this could have helped you to complete the Five Factor Test with increased insight as to the true motivations of your imminent counterparty.

To gain more insight as to the reality of the negotiation you are in, take the short Five Factor Test. The higher the level of each of these factors in your negotiation, the more likely it is that you are in a partnership and value-driven collaboration. The lower these factors, the more likely it is you are in a short-term, win/lose, competitive negotiation. As with everything, knowledge is key.

Mapping the issues

Your next step should be to brainstorm all of the possible issues that could be negotiated as part of the deal. This is a key step for ensuring that when you do get to the negotiation table, you are well prepared, have proposals planned in advance and can unlock all of the available value associated with this deal. This stage also encourages us to think broadly.

As we have already looked at in Chapter Two, we have a tendency to only focus in on the obvious issues – or the ones that we know really matter to *us*. This can limit the effectiveness of our preparation in terms of not fully considering all of our potential options to secure value. It can throw us off during the negotiation if we are suddenly presented with an issue we hadn't realised was important.

So, at this very early stage you should complete something like a Variable Mapper. This brainstorming exercise is designed to help you think broadly about all of the possible issues that could be negotiated as part of the deal you are about to do: everything that could be traded, whether big or small, cheap or expensive, short- or long-term, potentially valuable to you or to them, tangible or intangible. Even if you perceive it to be irrelevant, if it's something that could be negotiated between the parties, then jot it down in the mapper. You could write the issues down in a simple list, or you could this visual as a guide, populating each circle with a potential issue. The aim is simply to get all the issues written down and in one place.

VARIABLE MAPPER: What are the issues?

At this stage we are merely mapping the issues to understand the potential parameters of the deal. We are not assigning value or priority to either side. That will come in the next phase of the DEALS method – Establish.

The mapping process is there to protect you. It may seem excessive, but it is there to ensure that you have thought about every possible factor related to your future negotiation. A clever negotiator leaves nothing to chance. A clever negotiator doesn't leave themself vulnerable to attack, confusion or misinterpretation. They are prepared, full of useful information and brimming with creative insight.

I always say to my delegates on workshops that my strategy before a negotiation is to plan for every conceivable situation. From the absolute worst case scenario all the way through to my gold-plated vision of success. Why? Because if I have already thought through how each scenario might make me think, feel or react, then I am better equipped both emotionally and practically if I am ever confronted with it.

Lawrence Susskind advocates a similar mentality in his book *Good for You, Great for Me*.[12] Susskind recommends undertaking extensive planning and preparation at the early stages to insulate your deal against 'predictable surprises'. The phrase really speaks for itself. Your planning and preparation should have been extensive and effective enough that you have pre-empted everything. Any potential issue, no matter how seemingly remote or abstract, should have already been considered, evaluated and filed appropriately in your bank of information. There should be no such thing as an actual surprise at the negotiation table.

Preconditioning

Before we move on to the next stage, I should mention preconditioning and how it can impact our negotiations. When carrying out your research, be wary of taking all of the information you find as absolute fact. This is particularly true when considering information that is seemingly 'easy to access' or has been put into the public domain by your counterparty. Also, be slightly wary of any information they might have provided on existing pricing, fees or rates, or on how they 'normally do things'.

The reason for this is that we have to be mindful of any preconditioning that might be going on. Sometimes in the run-up to a negotiation, one side will seek to feed certain bits of information to the other side if it's in their interests for their counterparty to believe it and then base the rest of their thinking on that particular premise.

What could preconditioning look like in reality?

- Your counterparty readily sharing information about their standard fees or terms and conditions in advance of the negotiation. As a result, you start to plan your proposals based on what you believe the financials are going to have to look like to get a deal done. This is a form of anchoring (see Mistake Ten) and could serve to limit your perception of what the figures in the deal could be.

- You hear a rumour that one of your customers is shedding suppliers who can't offer extended payment terms and is going in really tough on all existing partners. As a result, you go into the negotiation ready to make an immediate concession on payment terms in order to preserve the relationship.

- A utilities company comments in a press release that it has become more expensive in recent years to distribute their raw product, due to political instability in another country, increased regulation from domestic authorities and increasing transportation costs. Consumers begin to brace themselves for the inevitable increase in the cost of that particular utility in the coming months.

- A technology company announces that, due to such high demand for their new smartphone handset, they are going to have to impose a waiting list. Consumers immediately scrabble to sign onto the waiting list and start to pay sky-high prices on auction sites for new handsets that are already out on the market.

Preconditioning happens routinely both in business and in life more generally. It is the drip-feeding of information to either the wider market or targeted companies and individuals to create an expectation in their mind as to how a situation might look or unfold over time. In negotiation terms, it can serve to distort the actual boundaries of the deal, so that our view on what could be possible is heavily influenced in their favour.

Of course, it is not always easy to know whether you are being preconditioned or not. This is because your counterparty (as with lying!) is highly unlikely to reveal to you upfront that this is what they are doing. As with everything in negotiation, make sure that you retain an element of cynicism and remain willing to question and challenge all of the information that you are provided with. If a piece of information comes too easily or you feel that it has been fed to you to influence your thinking (listen to your gut), just be prepared to think more broadly on that particular point. Question why they might want to influence you on that point and ensure that the next stage of your planning is not too heavily influenced by the information that has been provided to you, either directly or indirectly.

Before you move on to the next stage:

- Do you have enough information in your Insight Locker?

- Are there any gaps in your knowledge?

- Do you know what type of negotiation you are in?

- Have you mapped out all of the possible issues to be negotiated?

- Have you considered whether or not you have been preconditioned or whether you need to do some preconditioning of your own?

CHAPTER FOUR

Establish

Assumption is the enemy of amazing outcomes.

The next stage in the DEALS method is to Establish. Now that you have identified all the possible issues, this phase is about understanding which issues are priorities for each party, then working out your breakpoint, or 'walk away point', on every issue. Once you have a clear picture of this, you can establish the likely 'Negotiation Zone' where you will be able to get the deal done.

The previous phase was about broadly mapping out the issues and gathering all of the relevant information and detail that might influence the overall outcome of the deal. We are now starting to refine and understand the issues and what they might *mean* to each side.

What matters to each side?

When we were mapping out the potential issues in the negotiation, I mentioned that a common mistake people make is to focus solely on the issues that matter to them (see also Mistake Nine). This is one of the fastest ways to limit your success at the negotiation table. My mantra is this:

Different things mean different things to different people.

Not everyone will prioritise the same things. People are different. Companies are different. Countries are different. And as a result of this, they may well have very different needs, ideas, interpretations and requests. It is essential therefore that we work out exactly what it is that makes them tick. Get inside their head. See the world through their eyes and start to understand exactly what each issue in the negotiation means to them. Of course, in the previous phase of the DEALS method, you would have started to explore these things. You would have done your research, spoken to people in the know and reviewed any publicly available information out there.

But now it's time to up the ante. It's time to start to really understand who they are, how they think and what success and failure looks like to them. And if the situation allows it and the circumstances are appropriate, who better to explore this with than your counterparty themselves?

What?! Actually talk to my counterparty? Ask them what matters to them?

Yes. If appropriate. And while you're at it, you should also give them some insight into what matters to you too.

But surely disclosing all of that information will make us look vulnerable? Right?

Well, it depends. We have already explored the fact that not all negotiations are the same. Some will be inherently more competitive and some inherently more collaborative. Some will be very simple and transactional, some will be very creative and flexible. Some will be about value claiming and some will be about value creation. The point is that different negotiations require a different response, not just while you are at the negotiation table but also in how you conduct yourself during your planning phases and in how you engage with your counterparty prior to the event.

For example, if you are buying a car, you can more easily anticipate the salesman's priorities (price) and recognise your own (price, speed of sale). This transaction is very much about value claiming. As a result, you are more likely to play your cards close to your chest, act in a more stand-offish, reserved manner and push quite hard, as you know there is no long-term relationship to be preserved.

However, if you are negotiating with a potential partner for a ten-year joint venture and there are numerous issues to be traded and negotiated, then your priorities – and, consequently, your approach – are likely to be very different. You will be seeing these people again. Trust is going to be key. If you can both ensure each side feels sat-isfied with the outcome at the start of the interaction, you are less likely to have lingering resentment or unhappi-ness, or experience bumps in the road. In addition, in this kind of environment where you are looking to trade on a number of different issues, you really do need to under-stand what their priorities are. Otherwise, how can you ever work out how to effectively incentivise them?

In this scenario, it would be in your interests to engage in open dialogue. Of course, you might not be able to reveal absolutely everything you think or know for legal, ethical, commercial or data protection reasons, but if you can share it, you should. The more you understand each other the more you can jointly construct a deal that meets each side's needs.

How to understand your counterparty

How do you go about opening dialogue in advance of a more collaborative negotiation? These questions can give you a starting point:

What does success look like to you?
What are your plans?
What are your priorities?
How could we help you?

There is always a looming danger if you don't take the time to understand what matters to your counterparty, and that is that you make automatic assumptions that they share the same values as you (remember Mistake Nine); or you assume that they care about things that are really of very little consequence to them. As a result, you send the message at the negotiation table that you just don't take them seriously. So, if the deal is one that goes beyond just a short-term, competitive haggle, take the time to let them know that you want to understand them. It will prove hugely beneficial later on.

Making inaccurate assumptions can also cause major issues in terms of how able you are to construct proposals. It is essential that you understand the priorities of all sides if you are to extract the most value from the deal. This leads us on very nicely to the concepts of 'Takes' and 'Gives'.

Establish your 'Takes' and 'Gives'

A cornerstone of effective negotiation is understanding the benefits of trading. Trading in a negotiation allows us to look at what issues are on the table, identify what matters to each side and then establish a way of using these different issues to build an outcome that allows both to get what they want.

In some negotiations, the trade-off will be obvious. An artist has a painting that you want. You have some cash that the artist wants. Here is an obvious trade. But not all negotiations are that simple. When there is a bit more complexity to the deal it is imperative that you have understood which issues are particularly important to them (issues on which you might be prepared to give) and which ones are particularly important to you (issues on which you will need to take).

Why establish the importance of each issue? So that you can identify what you can do for them in order to help you achieve what you need. Do not underestimate the power of reciprocity in negotiation. If you can help them achieve what they need, they will be far more likely to assist you in achieving what you need. (For more on reciprocity, see Chapter Nine on the psychology of negotiation.) But, of course, you can only do this if you can develop appropriate trades.

This is where the concept of Takes and Gives comes in. You need to look at each issue and establish whether it is a Take or a Give. For this exercise, the more insight you have into your counterparty the better. The simple test you can carry out for each issue is to ask yourself, based on the information you have: is this a Take or a Give? Then go on to test your decision by analysing the impact on each party of giving or receiving the variable.

Take – something you need from them.
Give – something you can do for them.

The Issues Analysis tool opposite can be used to establish the impact of each Take and Give and the viability of each potential trade. For each issue, consider who wants it, why and the impact or cost to either side. For example, if something is high-impact or expensive for you to give but of low impact and interest to them, why would you offer it as an incentive? It makes no commercial sense.

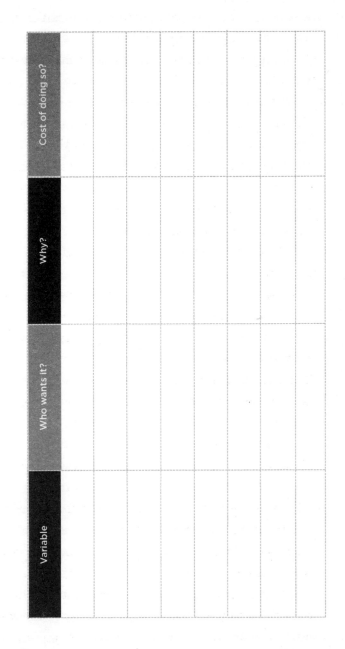

ISSUES ANALYSIS: Do you understand each side's priorities?

Variable	Who wants it?	Why?	Cost of doing so?

However, if you identify something you can offer to them that is affordable or manageable for you to give and that they really want ... that's the magic formula. We call that low-impact/high-impact trading.

In the next phase we will explore how to use Takes and Gives to help you construct proposals that will build and unlock value and opportunity in your negotiation, while at the same time preserving your bottom line and position.

Breakpoints and the Negotiation Zone

Once you have identified your Takes and Gives and *before* you start to draft your proposals, you need to start to understand the parameters of the deal you are about to do. This is essential so that you understand just what might be possible if you manage the process well, but also so that you can preserve your profit margin, position or bottom line. For each issue that could be traded (as mapped out in the earlier phase), you will need to establish each party's breakpoint.

What is a breakpoint? Your breakpoint is, quite simply, your bottom line, your worst-case scenario or your safety net. As the buyer, it is the absolute maximum you will pay, and as the seller, it is the absolute minimum you would accept. It is called your breakpoint because it is the point at which if you go higher or lower, then the deal is not viable.

It is often pretty obvious to you what your breakpoint will be. You should know your case, your market, your value, your position and your financials; so, as a result, you should be able to correctly identify your breakpoint on every issue. That's the easy part. To be clear, your break-point should be your worst-case scenario. The point at which if you had to, you could do a deal ... but in reality you would rather achieve something better. But remember, in a worst-case scenario you could do a deal here.

Breaking your breakpoint

The breakpoint golden rule is that you stick to it. You might be tempted, in the heat of a negotiation and the desperation to get a deal, to pay just a little more or accept a little less than your breakpoint. But beware! An extra pound, dollar or euro here opens you up to a slippery scale of 'just another' there, and suddenly one dollar becomes two, two becomes three, and before you know it you are walking away with a deal that is worth far less than you can really afford to agree to.

What is often far trickier is thinking about your counter-party's breakpoint because, of course, it probably isn't going to be in their interest to reveal exactly what their breakpoint is. And also bear in mind, based on what we explored on opening ambitiously or testing the water in the CNM section, any figure that they tell you is their breakpoint, probably isn't.

Now of course, you could just take a wild guess ... or, you could gather together all of the available evidence you have and then get inside their head to try to see the world through their eyes. You could start to estimate their breakpoint based on current standard rates in your marketplace, based on what you have paid for similar services in the past, and based on what you know they have provided for previous clients.

But you should also go further. Start to understand that often there will be a number of factors influencing how far someone will go on a particular issue. Maybe they are under pressure from a third party? Maybe they have a tough deadline that is driving them to do this deal in a certain way? Maybe their cash flow is so poor it is influencing the rates they will work for? Maybe they are an avid collector and so would pay over the publicised market value to secure a certain product? Maybe they are looking to exit a certain market? Maybe they just want to close this deal quickly as they are going on their honeymoon in two days' time? Maybe they are trying to impress a new boss. You get the idea.

Any number of factors could be influencing what they might be willing to agree to and where they have set their breakpoint. Your job is not to assume that you automatically know their breakpoint but instead to adopt a curious mindset and explore how the world looks to them.

So, for each issue you need to:

- Set your breakpoint.

- Think creatively about what their breakpoint might be.

You can then go on to thinking about the possible boundaries of the deal and look at the Negotiation Zone. There are lots of different names given to the field in which a potential deal could be done: 'zone of potential agreement', 'bargaining range', 'trading zone' ... I am simply going to refer to it as the 'Negotiation Zone'.

The point of establishing this zone and mapping it out is to understand where you need to be steering the negotiation once you get to the deal table. The Negotiation Zone represents the point at which it's possible for a deal to be done. It is the point between each party's breakpoint on each issue, in which a deal would be acceptable to either side.

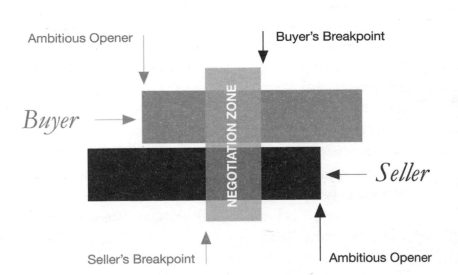

The simple model in this diagram plays out the Negotiation Zone in relation to one variable. For the sake of simplicity, let's say this variable is cost or price. You can see in the diagram that the Buyer's breakpoint has been set at £14. As a buyer, this represents the highest you could possibly go on this point.

After careful consideration and research, you, as the Buyer, have decided that you think the Seller's breakpoint is £10. This will represent the lowest amount that the Seller could possibly accept. You need to remember that this is simply an educated guess. In the next phase, we will explore why opening ambitiously is a good way of testing just how accurate you were in establishing the other party's breakpoint.

Of course, the aim of the game is to try to get the best possible outcome. As a result, you are going to try to finish closer to their breakpoint than to your own. In the diagram, a deal closer to £10 would be a better outcome for you as the Buyer than it would be for the Seller. By doing this, you will have been able to maximise the available Negotiation Zone.

Other key reference points in the Negotiation Zone, or Breakpoint Mapper, diagram are your Ambitious Opener (your starting proposal) and the Get Real Point (the shaded area beyond each party's Breakpoint). Both of these points have been explored in Chapter Two and will be revisited again in the Ask section of the DEALS method (Chapter Five).

When you are in a negotiation with multiple issues, it is often helpful to produce an overall map of the various breakpoints. This can act as a point of reference both before and during the negotiation. It will also allow you oversight of all of the possibilities in the deal. It is key that you have understood all of the issues fully, so you are going to have to analyse the breakpoints for each issue, even if there are hundreds of them. If you don't do this, you are never going to fully understand where you might be able to get to in this deal, and you could end up leaving bucketloads of value behind, because you haven't utilised the less obvious issues.

The Possibilities Plotter below shows how you can expand from looking at a single issue to the multiple issues in your deal. Here we have Takes (T) on the left and Gives (G) on the right. Each triangle represents an

POSSIBILITIES PLOTTER:
What are the boundaries for each variable?

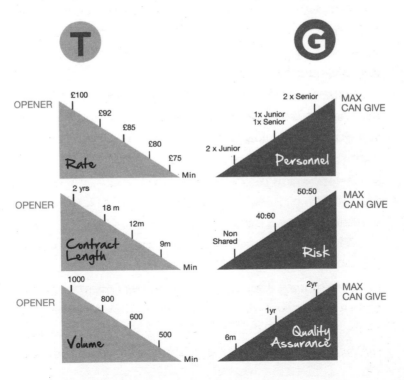

issue, such as the rate you charge, on which you should plot your breakpoint (the bottom-right of your Take triangles and the top-right of your Give triangles) and your best guess as to their breakpoint (the top-left of your Takes and the bottom-right of your Gives). These triangles now represent the likely boundaries of each negotiable issue in the deal.

What is the alternative?

As a final step in the Establish phase, you should fully consider what your alternatives are if you can't reach an agreement in the forthcoming negotiation. Do you have other options? Could you get the product somewhere else? Is your service in demand elsewhere? Can you afford to wait for another opportunity? For more on understanding your Best Alternative To Negotiated Agreement (BATNA) take a look at Chapter Eight on the Balance of Power. Whether or not you have credible and robust alternatives can make a huge difference to how you conduct a negotiation and how much power you really have at your disposal.

Before you move on, stop to reflect:

- Have you seen the world through their eyes?

- Have you exchanged relevant information?

- Have you established your Takes and Gives?

- Have you worked out each side's breakpoints on all of the possible trading issues?

CHAPTER FIVE

Ask

The next phase of the DEALS method is to assert yourself and ask. In the right way. This phase is primarily concerned with our conduct and behaviour during the negotiation. But before we get anywhere near the bargaining table, we are going to start by planning some proposals, or our 'asks'.

As I have said already, winging it is never a smart negotiation strategy. It is not sensible to turn up at the negotiation table and make it up as you go along. The chances are you will end up simply being led by the other side and constantly reacting to the proposals they make to you. Failing that, your mind will go blank and you will end up suggesting proposals that are really not that great once you pick apart the deal later on. (I routinely see even the most intelligent people lose their way in negotiations where they haven't prepared properly.)

It's a clever approach to have already planned a number of proposals before you get to the negotiation. All of the previous phases of the DEALS method will have now delivered you to the point where you have more than enough information to start preparing some robust and insightful proposals.

Proactive vs Reactive

The starting point for this section is to challenge what is a very commonly held concept for many people. On training programmes and during coaching, when I advise people to plan some proposals in advance, a common pushback is: 'But how can I do that when I don't know what they are going to propose to me?'

Without wishing to sound brutal: negotiation is not about you passively waiting to hear what their proposals might be. It is about you being smart enough to understand that their proposals are merely going to be exaggerated versions of what works for them. What you don't want to do is anchor to their proposals or get bogged down in them – which, if you haven't planned your own proposals in advance, you will inevitably do. So, do yourself a favour: research effectively, plan properly and get some proposals written before you get anywhere near that negotiation.

Look, you might not use all of them. You might use one or two, and skip a couple. But by having them there at least you have options and a possible route through the negotiation. This will be a lifesaver when the pressure is on and your nerves are going haywire.

If You ..., Then I ...

When you are planning your proposals you need to embrace – and I mean fully embrace – the construction 'If you ..., then I ...'.

Earlier in the book, I introduced the idea that this phrase is our saviour in preventing us from giving things away for free. By constructing our proposals in this way, we ensure that we are always getting something back in return. We are not just giving and giving and giving.

In the previous phase, we identified which of the issues in a negotiation were Takes and which were Gives. We also worked out what the breakpoints were for each party on each of the issues. It is now time to put this pre-work to good use.

Using the list of Gives and Takes, and taking on board the breakpoints for each issue, you should start to pair up which issues will form part of your proposals. Using this approach, you are going to be *asking* for your Take and then *offering* your Give in return. The message? I am more than happy to help you achieve what you need, but I am going to have to see that you are willing to help me too. You are going to have to work for this reward.

The Proposal Planner overleaf offers a simple table to help you structure your proposals effectively as 'If you ..., then I ...' trades.

One of the biggest obstacles that I witness at this point is that people get way too bogged down in over thinking what Take they should pair with what Give. They overanalyse what should go with what. But in truth, for the first few proposals it doesn't really matter that much.

PROPOSAL PLANNER: What are your moves going to be?

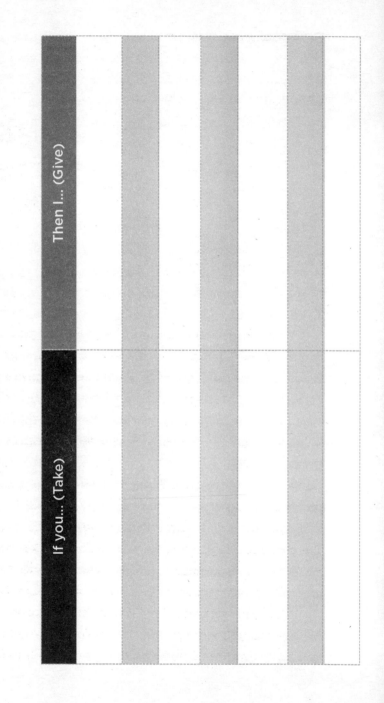

Proposal pick-and-mix

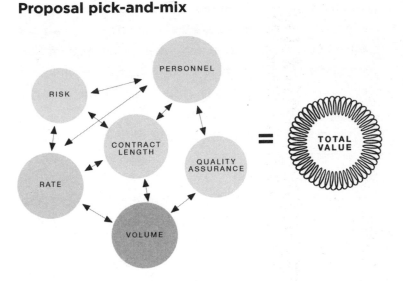

The Total Value diagram above illustrates the point that a multi-issue deal should be viewed as one in which you are trying to unlock as much total value and opportunity as possible. It also illustrates that total value is only accessible when you view all of the variables as integral to the deal, and when you explore each variable's potential trading options. This means that you should avoid working in the silo mentality of always pairing the same issues each time. If you adopt this very traditional mentality, you will find that, while you are able to agree on a number of initial points, as the deal unfolds you will find yourself being left with the more difficult, complex and controversial issues that you were always going to struggle to reach an agreement on.

When this occurs, if you deem that the other issues have already been agreed and are 'off the table', then you have limited options when it comes to levering an agreement on the more controversial matters. If you can't bring those 'agreed' issues back onto the table for review and an alternative agreement, then you end up swinging back to a hard bargaining mentality. And then you are most certainly limiting the deal you can do, as the interaction will start to feel more like a battle.

Instead, you need to retrain your brain to see the deal in its entirety. Look across all of the issues and view each one as being potentially linked to any of the others. I call this pick-and-mix trading, where you can pair any of the issues together to try to maximise the value associated with each of them.

POSSIBILITIES PLOTTER:
What can be traded?

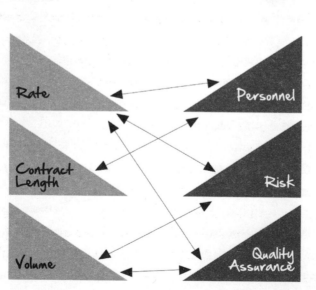

Having talked about all of the work we have to do before we get to the negotiation table, the following tips are designed to help you with making the 'ask' once you are in the negotiation.

Don't get bogged down by reactionary responses
One of the things that you need to do is ensure that every move you make is not just a direct response to what they have proposed to you. Say, for example, that they propose:

> *'If you can pay £500, then we can guarantee the product by next Wednesday.'*

Do not be tempted to then focus on discussing this until you have thrashed out an agreement on just those two issues. This is particularly true if you actually have no intention of ever accepting the proposal. If you spend too much time 'responding' to their proposal, you are merely anchoring yourself to what they have asked for.

Instead, follow your plan. Suggest an alternative proposal that you have drafted in advance. You might want to think about phrases such as:

> *'Thanks for that suggestion. That's not something we could agree to, but what we could agree to is ...'*

And make them feel heard. As we have already identified, people like to feel heard. They want their opinions and suggestions to be taken seriously. They don't want to have their ideas dismissed outright. So, you can help soften the fact that you are moving on from their proposal to making your own, by making sure that any proposal you make builds on what they just asked for.

If you have followed the phases of the DEALS method and completed the Proposal Planner (page 126) and the Breakpoint Mapper (page 119), you should have a compendium of potential options for proposals right at your fingertips. It should, therefore, be relatively easy for you to respond to their proposal by acknowledging some of the points made while still ensuring you are presenting proposals that meet your objectives.

So how would this work in practice? Imagine that your counterparty makes the offer we just mentioned:

> *'If you can pay £500, then we can guarantee the product by next Wednesday.'*

You should then look at your tools, select a pre-planned proposal based on one of the points they made, or select relevant issues from the Breakpoint Mapper and respond with:

> *'Thanks for that proposal. Looking at the bigger picture, we would struggle with that. But I like the idea of working towards Wednesday ... So, how about: if you can guarantee delivery by Wednesday, we could offer you £440 and a written testimonial.'*

This way you are able to use their proposal as a foundation

for your response, but you are still talking about what you want while politely moving on from their suggestion. This whole approach requires flexibility. To be able to do this, you will have to have understood all of the different issues and where you might be able to go on them well in advance. So don't skimp on the proposals you prepare in advance. You might not use all of them, but to have a number of options in front of you that you can use, modify or come back to is incredibly empowering.

Back-pocket strategy

Of course, in any multi-issue negotiation there may be certain points that you want to get out on the table early and others that you might want to hang on to for greater impact later on. If you are going to do this, it's essential that you highlight which issues will warrant special treatment early on in this proposal drafting stage and make sure that anyone you are negotiating alongside, or for, is clear on why you are adopting this strategy.

Don't offer it all at once!

When making your proposals, make sure that you don't offer the maximum on each issue immediately. Make them work for it! That way you can ensure you have got everything you need before you give up everything you have to trade with. When constructing your proposals you should initially *ask big* and *offer small*. That way you can make the other party feel like they are winning when later in the negotiation you offer something *bigger* on that issue than you did initially.

Get real!

Of course, you have to be mindful of the 'Get Real Point' (see page 76) when making your initial proposals. Don't open so ambitiously that your proposal is ridiculous or unrealistic. This is particularly true if trust and collaboration will be key components of any future agreement. There is a difference between ambitious and outlandish.

Use time-outs if you lose focus

If things start to get muddled, you have lost track of your position, or you have simply run out of proposals and have found yourself becoming too reactionary or winging it, a good tactic is to call a time-out.

Negotiations are often tense, stressful and demanding, even in the most collaborative of situations. A time-out can be a great way for you and any team members to take a deep breath, review where you have got to and plan where you want to go next. A time-out is not a sign of weakness. You should view it as an informed gap in the proceedings for both you and your counterparty to make sure you are on course for an agreement. If you have followed all of the phases in the DEALS method before you get to the negotiation, planning some new proposals in the time-out should be as simple as reviewing your tools and, based on your progress, drafting some new 'If you ..., then I ...' statements to guide you through the next part of the meeting.

Remember: try to go first, if you can

We have already discussed in some detail the importance of anchoring and making the first proposal. The evidence behind going first is plentiful, compelling and should not be ignored. If you can make the first proposal then you should try to.

Do be aware that your counterparty might try sneakily to use anchoring by sending you their opening proposal in advance. If this does happen, simply make sure that you are not too swayed by what their proposal contains. Review it, make a note, but stick to your pre-prepared plan of proposals while using their opening proposal for some insight into how they might be approaching the wider negotiation.

Remember

Their opening proposal is simply an exaggerated version of what works for them, from their perspective. Don't let that impact your plan ... unless you spot something that you hadn't anticipated which works in your favour. If that's the case, take a moment to wonder why the deal might be too good to be true, or scold yourself for having not pre-empted it. Remember the concept of predictable surprises (see page 105).

Prepare for going second

Of course, you might be in a negotiation where industry ritual or process demands that your counterparty go first.

Or they might simply get in there straightaway with the first proposal. In this instance, don't panic. The negotiation isn't doomed to fail because they have made the first move.

Instead, *recognise* the power of anchoring and the potential impact of making the first offer. Then, make sure that you don't reinforce it by making the mistakes highlighted in Chapter Two, especially:

* Don't dwell on it
* Don't argue about it
* Don't ask them to explain themselves.

Instead, you should simply acknowledge the offer, thank them for it and move on. Then start talking about what you *can* do. Cast out a new anchor: make *your* proposal the response.

Let's recap before you move on. Have you:

* Adopted a proactive, rather than a reactive, mindset when it comes to making your 'ask'?

* Planned using the If you ..., then I ... mantra?

* Utilised all of the different issues when constructing your proposals?

* Thought about how to deal with anchoring?

* Been mindful of the Get Real Point?

* Planned to open ambitiously and first?

CHAPTER SIX

Lead

This next phase is concerned purely with the negotiation itself. Or, more importantly, with whether we are controlling the negotiation or letting it control us.

The impact of your previous mapping, planning and plotting could be severely reduced if you do not take the lead in the negotiation. Taking the lead means being in control. Executing the deal brilliantly. Managing the negotiation. Managing any team members with you. Managing the environment. But also, managing yourself.

What we say and what we do

We have already talked about the fact that many people find negotiation pretty tough. Sure, there are some people who really love the whole process, but many others will find it awkward, difficult and a real challenge.

It's no secret that when human beings experience stress, nerves or anxiety, we become flooded with adrenaline. Our heart beats faster, our guts churn, our breathing quickens and we generally feel on edge. Our fight-or-flight mentality will shape how we respond to the people around us. All of this will begin to have an impact on how we start to interact and communicate with others. Often, the best way to see what someone is thinking about something is to listen and watch for the things they say and the things they do.

Of course, many people are aware of this response and will invest time and money in learning how to mask their nerves, stress, anxiety, fear or anger. There are some people out there who are incredibly skilled at presenting the appropriate mask or performance. An obvious example is professional poker players, for whom the ability to maintain calm in a high-stakes environment is of fundamental importance to their success.

But not everyone is a professional poker player: not everyone is skilled at controlling the verbal and non-verbal messages they give out. On our training programmes, my team and I use video technology to show people how easy they are to read in a high-pressure negotiation. Of course, we also show them how to read the same kinds of messages coming from their counterparty.

The point is: you need to make sure that you are in control of your whole self during a negotiation. You need to be conscious of the language you are using and the message it's really sending, as well as being in control of your physical 'tells' and 'giveaways'.

Controlling your physical tells

- Use breathing to calm yourself.
- Count to five in your mind before answering a challenging question.
- Try to speak more slowly.
- Use firm language.
- Be conscious of your movements: don't fiddle and fidget.
- Feel grounded by planting both feet on the floor.
- Sit tall.

Agenda

A really simple way of making sure that you retain an element of control and are able to lead a negotiation is to suggest the use of agendas, both in the run-up to and during the negotiation. This could cover everything from what will be discussed in any pre-meets through to where the negotiation will take place, how long it will last, and who will be present and in what capacity. By sharing this beforehand and developing it together, each side feels involved and engaged in the process.

This also gives you a great get-out clause if they spring something unexpected on you during the negotiation or seek to change the rules of engagement. If both sides have been working to a shared agenda and your counterparty throws an unforeseen issue or 'rule' into the mix, you can politely and professionally say:

'We prepared for this meeting on the basis of the agenda we jointly developed. Because this wasn't raised earlier in the process, we haven't considered it. I would like to be able to give this my full attention and request a time-out in order for us to explore the issue further, both with you and as a team.'

Capture the deal

In a multi-issue deal, managing complexity and tracking your progress on areas of agreement as the deal unfolds can be a real challenge. One of the easiest ways to keep track of the negotiation and to make sure that all issues are being effectively utilised is to use a Deal Sheet.

A tool such as the Deal Sheet is incredibly simple yet powerful as it allows you to capture the progress being made, and to identify areas where you might be stalling or where you simply haven't prepared enough proposals. It is also useful in that it prevents you from slipping back into the silo mentality (always pairing the same issues each time instead of adopting a flexible, pick-and-mix approach).

The Deal Sheet works by capturing every proposal that is made against every issue. There is no way of tracking which issue is paired with what each time. Instead, what you see as the negotiation progresses is a simple visual of the areas where you appear to be in agreement and also those areas where you still have distance between you. It provides you with 'real-time' data on each issue. And because it gathers all the issues together, you can consider the deal in its entirety. You start to move

DEAL SHEET: Record the deal as it unfolds

Variable	Your move	Their move	Your move	Their move	Your move	Their move	Your move	Their move	Your move	Their move	Your move
Unit Price	100,000	64,000	98,500	72,350	91,750						
Delivery	60 days	21 days	50 days								
Sign off level	Manager	Partner	Manager	Director	Director						
Referral	Yes	Yes									
Penalty	5%	30%	9%	22%	15%	20%	15%				
Contract Length	4 years	6 months									

away from focusing only on the obvious issues. This is essential, as it means that you limit the chance of leaving any value behind. You are able to see which issues could still be used to stimulate progression or agreement, and you are also able to see whether you have got a great deal overall.

One of the dangers of not negotiating in this way is that you focus on securing agreement on the big, high-profile items first. So, for example, you might target getting an agreement early on in relation to pricing. After a bit of to-ing and fro-ing on a couple of issues, you finally agree on what looks to be a pretty good deal for you. However, as the rest of the deal unfolds, you find that because some of your most important issues have been put aside as agreed, you have less to use as a lever. You remain upbeat though because you have a good outcome on pricing. You trundle though the rest of the deal, and after shaking hands you retreat to examine the outcome. It's only upon reviewing the deal in its entirety that you realise you have got a good outcome on price at the cost of a shorter contract, a lengthy wait for your invoices to be paid, excessive expectations on seniority of personnel and a restrictive exclusivity clause. All of a sudden, that agreement on pricing doesn't seem so attractive after all.

Instead of this, start to think in terms of overall value. All of the issues in negotiation should be viewed as interwoven. Adopting a 'complete package', or 'pick-and-mix', approach rather than addressing issues in isolation will help you both to protect yourself and to wring as much value out of the deal as possible.

Nothing is agreed until everything is agreed

To assist you with adopting the complete package approach, you should heed the mantra frequently used in international trade and diplomacy negotiations: 'Nothing is agreed until everything is agreed.' This mantra is all about ensuring that each side understands that the deal needs to be agreed in its entirety before any final sign-off.

Sometimes you will find yourself negotiating with someone who frequently interjects when you are making proposals with something like:

> 'Hang on a minute, I thought we had agreed on a deadline of November for this project?'
> 'You mentioned earlier on that we would get ten people on the project, and now you are saying nine?'

A simple response to someone who seems intent on swinging the deal back round the silo approach is to suggest that 'nothing is agreed until everything is agreed'. This will help to defuse any possible 'he said …, she said …' or bickering about people having misunderstood each other.

The Holding Pen

In addition to this mantra, one of the ways to ensure that the negotiation can progress and unfold without getting bogged down in complexity is to agree issues in principle throughout the interaction. One of the tools that my team uses is the 'Holding Pen', a virtual space off the table where issues agreed in principle can be parked in order to ease congestion in the ongoing negotiation.

So, if you have reviewed your Deal Sheet during a time-out and have seen that both sides seem to be proposing something similar on a number of issues, upon re-entering the negotiation you could say something like:

> 'We had a look at where we have got to so far, and we can see that we appear to be speaking the same language on Issues A, B, C and D. As a result, we would suggest that we place those issues in the Holding Pen for now as agreed in principle, but subject to agreement on all of the other issues. Of course, if we find we are struggling later on, we can always bring those issues back out of the Holding Pen and review them.'

The Holding Pen could be a completely abstract and intangible concept, or you could decide to use a flipchart populated with Post-It notes of the issues. I would advise that you suggest the use of the Holding Pen well before you get into the nitty gritty of the deal; that way you can embed a shared understanding of why it would be useful for both sides.

Discipline in the team

If you are negotiating as part of a team, one of the most important things to do is make sure that everyone in the team is clear on their role, what is expected of them, and what they can and cannot do.

It is not uncommon to see the members of a negotiating team undermine themselves by talking over each other, unwittingly contradicting each other or even making things up as they go along. Of course, if you are negotiating against well-trained professionals they will notice this and take it as a sign that you are not a cohesive and unified team. As a result, they may try to encourage loose tongues, single out weaker team members or just confuse you further by challenging what the team is actually asking for.

Protect yourself from this kind of unruliness by assigning roles to your team members before you get to the negotiation. You might want to consider assigning someone as the Communicator to deliver the pre-planned proposals; someone as the Analyst to fill out the Deal Sheet and plan possible proposals; someone as the Interpreter to read the other side, listening carefully for clues and insight and supporting the Analyst in seeing how the deal is unfolding; and finally someone as the Diplomat to manage climate control, making introductions, smoothing over difficult issues and keeping the room focused and positive. Ultimately, the Diplomat should also be empowered to make decisions on behalf of the group.

Team roles

Communicator: Acts as the spokesperson for the group. Delivers the pre-planned proposals clearly and succinctly.

Analyst: Uses the Deal Sheet to record the deal as it unfolds. Has a full understanding of the breakpoints and is able to plan new proposals.

Interpreter: Monitors the people in the room, reads signals and listens for clues. Supports the Analyst by interpreting how the deal is unfolding and suggests alternative proposals to keep the team on track.

Diplomat: Keeps the negotiation moving. Manages the climate in the room, smoothing over negativity and barriers. Is empowered to commit to the deal at the end.

Climate control and the Diplomat

In a high-pressure, multi-issue negotiation there are bound to be tensions, differences of opinion and sticky areas where agreement seems challenging. This is true in even the most solid of relationships and collaborative of approaches. If there is a relationship to be maintained post-agreement, or if you simply are of the view that a more collaborative approach will be more beneficial than an aggressive one, it makes sense to assign someone in the team to regulate the room's climate.

At the start of the interaction, this person should ensure that introductions are made, and that everyone is comfortable and has what they need. The Diplomat should also make some kind of opening statement in relation to the intention of each side to reach a productive agreement. They should take responsibility for ensuring that roles are observed within their team and for managing fraying tempers or situations where people are becoming stuck on difficult issues.

There is a famous expression that any Diplomat would benefit from bearing in mind: *the iron hand in the velvet glove.* The thrust of the expression is that you can be tough and firm on the issues (the iron hand), but you need to remain warm and soft on the people if you are to maintain a relationship (the velvet glove).

As the person managing the climate, it is your job to remain tough and focused on the issues throughout the negotiation, but also to preserve and even advance the relationship. To help you with this, pull together a bank of statements that could help the negotiation to progress should you face difficult issues that drag each side away from agreement. We call these 'words that soothe and phrases that move'. An example of good climate control could be:

> *'We are making great strides here, and I feel like we are getting closer to consensus on a number of really important points. As there appear to be some strong views here, how about we take a breather on this one for now and come back to it after we've had a look at some of the issues we haven't yet addressed?'*

The first part includes the 'words that soothe': you are reminding people how much has been achieved and that agreement is not far off. The second part is a 'phrase that moves': by suggesting that you look at alternative issues before coming back to the point of disagreement, you can defuse any growing tension and clear the air before returning to it, hopefully with fresh eyes all round.

Progress summaries

If you are negotiating a particularly complex deal with lots of different issues, it can be incredibly easy for the parties around the table to become confused, misunderstand each other and lose track of where they have got to in the negotiation.

A simple way to limit the risk of this happening and potentially derailing the negotiation is to use progress summaries throughout. This allows the parties to review what has been agreed in principle and what still needs to be addressed, and to identify areas where there appears to be a sticking point (so that each side can start to come up with ways to overcome it in their next proposals). The Deal Sheet can be used to help with this, as it provides an at-a-glance summary of where you are on each of the issues from each side's perspective. This can help you plan the direction of your next proposals more effectively.

In addition, regular summaries can help to protect the deal from tumbling all the way back to the beginning because of mistakes or misinterpretation. I have heard about numerous deals that fell through because of a misunderstanding that was embedded into the deal in the early stages and that only became apparent right at the end when the deal was being summarised.

Tick-tock

If you are to remain in control and take the lead in your negotiation, it is essential that you're aware of one of the most commonly used tactics in negotiation: the manipulation of time.

How often have you gone into a meeting only to be told that the planned 50 minutes has to be condensed to twenty minutes but that you still need to get a deal done today? Or that you only have 24 hours to give your response to a complex proposal? Or that an important negotiation has moved, such that you only have 48 hours to prepare rather than a week? Or that an important negotiation has been delayed and delayed, and you are under a pressing deadline on the issue from another source? Or that if you don't agree to your counterparty's proposal in the next five minutes they're going to go talk to an alternative supplier who is ready to do a deal?

Time is a strange thing. For something so universally regulated, it has a strange habit of appearing to speed up or slow down when we least want it to. You can probably remember a date that seemed to pass agonisingly slowly when you realised that you really didn't like the person and just wanted it to end ... Or the two-week holiday of a lifetime that seemed to fly by in a flash when you desperately hoped it would never end.

It is often said that nothing focuses the mind like a looming deadline. In fact, one of the things I have observed in many different negotiation settings is that when the clock is ticking, people often focus too much on their fear of failure or of deadlocking. It is this fear that often results in people agreeing to things that they would never normally agree to. In the heat of the moment, with your counterparty saying, 'Come on! We don't have long. We do a deal today or not at all!', the pressure to just say 'yes' can be overwhelming.

Similarly, if you haven't been given enough time to research and understand the issues in a negotiation, many people would rather be swept along and agree to something that sounds OK on the surface rather than halt proceedings and say, 'You know what? I don't think I'm happy with this. I need more time to review the information.'

Be aware of time. Keep a track of it. Challenge reductions in time made available to you. Question and resist excessive delays. Ask why a deadline has been set and query whether there could be flexibility. In short, be in control of the time, rather than letting it take control of you.

Have a strategy for dealing with challenging behaviour

One of the biggest obstacles to remaining calm and in control in a negotiation is other people's challenging behaviour. I'm talking about the negotiator who:

- Talks over you

- Is rude

- Is overly aggressive

- Invades your personal space

- Constantly rejects your proposals without offering alternatives

- Uses threats.

All of these examples can be hugely intimidating during a negotiation and if unanticipated can come as a huge shock to you if you had been planning on adopting a collaborative and professional approach. You can have prepared diligently, planned plenty of proposals and fully briefed your team, but of all that can amount to nothing if you are derailed or upset by these kinds of behaviours.

I would like to be able to tell you that these kinds of behaviours aren't used regularly, but unfortunately they are, and often as part of a very deliberate and pre-planned strategy. In 95 per cent of cases these behaviours are little more than a tactic to throw you off track, make you vulnerable and increase your perception of their power. The remaining 5 per cent involve either nasty bullies or parties with so much power and influence that they really don't care about playing hardball because they know they have plenty of alternatives waiting in the wings.

Challenging behaviours can result in negative implications for your deal, particularly if you are unprepared for them or intimidated by them. I have dedicated a whole section of this book, Part Four, to understanding and dealing with obstacles; if you encounter these kinds of behaviours and they pose a problem for you, take a detailed look at those chapters.

You can often minimise these behaviours or tactics by:

- Pre-empting them and planning in advance how you are going to respond

- Thinking about why they feel the need to behave this way; it is often a direct result of trying to mask or deflect from inadequacies

- Ignoring them – it often takes the wind out of their sails

- Calling them out – the alternative to the previous tip, sometimes this can deflate the challenging behaviour completely.

A clever negotiator knows that maintaining a cool, calm and confident edge during deals can help you remain in control no matter what your counterparty throws at you. Remember, by being in charge of your negotiation you can help to steer it more effectively to where you need it to end. If you don't lead ... guess what? They will. And the direction of their steer will, of course, be very much in their favour.

Final points before you move on:

- Have you developed a strategy for dealing with your nerves?

- Are you and your counterparty working to a joint agenda?

- Are you utilising the Deal Sheet?

- Nothing is agreed until everything is agreed. Have you suggested using the Holding Pen?

- Do you have a designated Diplomat for climate control?

- Are you in charge of time?

- Have you planned how you will deal with challenging behaviour?

CHAPTER SEVEN

Seal

The handshake is often just the start.

The final phase of the DEALS method is how to effectively seal the deal. A great many people fall into the trap of thinking that the hard work is done and the negotiation is over once you sign on the dotted line or shake hands. Wrong.

In my experience, some of the most complex aspects of a negotiation take place after a deal has been agreed. It is essential that the deal you do is constructed in such a way that it protects you and your interests post-agreement. You need to ensure that you have given yourself room to review and exit in case of poor performance or non-delivery or to renegotiate terms in case of a change in circumstance or requirement.

Near-end summary

As you approach the end of a negotiation, it is essential that you don't drown in complexity and detail. Clarity is key as the close of a deal draws near because this is the point at which any misunderstandings or differences of opinion are likely to rear up, since each side realises they are running out of chances to lock in everything that they need.

As it starts to become clear that a deal isn't far off, a wise tactic is to summarise the deal as it currently stands from your perspective. By doing this, you can remind people of how far you have come (see Chapter Six on why this is useful) and you can signal to the other side any areas where agreement still eludes you.

Once any outstanding issues have been addressed, do make sure that you summarise again, right before deal closure. You want to be absolutely certain that you have fully understood the deal in its entirety. To avoid the potential of any later confusion or pushback, ask your counterparty if this is also their understanding of the deal as it stands. You should only shake hands when you are fully satisfied that you have reached an agreement on every single issue on the table.

Congratulations! We have a deal! ... Or do we?

Post-deal, pre-paperwork

There will often be a period of time between the agreement of a deal, as marked by the shaking of hands, and the signing of formal contracts. If not managed correctly, this is the period of time when you could start to see the deal you thought you had agreed being eroded, chipped away at or potentially changed beyond all recognition.

It's also a time in which many people are unclear about both their personal rights and, from a corporate perspective, the enforceability of the deal they have just finalised. The rules governing whether or not your hand-shake or verbal agreement is binding will vary depending on the legal jurisdiction in which you are operating, the type of product or service you have just purchased or sold, or the nature of the negotiation you have just completed. To check this, as an individual, a good place to research your position would be a consumer rights or consumer law website. For a corporation involved in a negotiation with significant operational, financial and reputational implications, you would be wise to seek advice from the relevant regional legal counsel.

Is a handshake legally binding?

It depends! Whether or not a handshake is considered legally binding will vary from jurisdiction to jurisdiction. However, it is worth recognising that in many parts of the world it is the *specificity* of the agreement that is likely to influence a judge – that is, is the subject of the discussion vague? Or is it crystal clear what each side was referring to and on what terms? Did each party had the intention to create a legally binding contract, and can this be evidenced in any way?

To help solidify the deal, bear the following tips in mind:

- Consider having each side sign a written agreement 'in principle' document, as a precursor to the formal contract.

- Ensure a handshake or verbal agreement is witnessed by a third party.

- Agree a defined time period during which each side can come back and query or challenge what has been agreed.

- Arrange for the parties to maintain contact between the close of the deal and contract signature to keep the relationship on the right track.

- Be mindful of criticising your counterparty and the deal in public before the contract is signed.

- Be cautious of overly celebrating your 'victory' if you have just secured the 'deal of a lifetime'. You don't want them to start to feel that the deal is one they might want to back out of ...

Future-proofing the deal

When you are finalising the agreement, make sure to 'future-proof' it. In the excitement of closing a deal which means a lot to you or your company, you may find that the last thing you want to think about is the deal failing, one side not delivering to a required standard, or the two sides just not working well together. However, this is exactly when you should be thinking about failure! Your formal agreement should incorporate a number of protections and safety nets just in case things do go sour. Even if the agreed deal doesn't break down catastrophically, these safety nets will help maintain the relationship because everyone is clear about where they stand and what is expected of them.

Clear and succinct

Make sure that the terms of your agreement are clear and succinct to avoid confusion or doubt. Try not to overcomplicate the agreement with jargon and convoluted language, and make sure that representatives on both sides are involved in approving and signing off any final contract, memorandum or deal summary. You want to avoid either side claiming they didn't know what they were signing up to or that you had unrealistic expectations if the deal starts to face problems.

Make sure that the agreement includes clear guidance in relation to performance indicators, escalation procedures, trigger points and what is deemed to be acceptable or unacceptable conduct. You should leave no room for doubt as to what success and failure look like and how you will jointly approach dealing with bumps in the road or failure.

Regular review

Your agreement should also include the requirement for regular review, both informal and formal. Informal review might be a commitment to speak on the phone on a regular, defined basis to discuss progress. Formal review might mean quarterly governance meetings that appraise the whole deal and address bigger or strategic challenges that present themselves.

The point is, make sure that the lines of communication between the parties in the deal remain open and accessible. If you regularly share information you will be far better prepared to anticipate any major problems on the horizon.

Things change

If your deal is an ongoing one or covers a period of multiple years, you should incorporate terms that allow for
re-negotiation of key aspects of the deal, either at a set
point in time (e.g. two years into a four-year deal) or trig-
gered by certain situations (e.g. interest rates hitting a
defined point or the introduction of new technology).

The fact is that things change, and your deal needs
to have the flexibility to move with the times. A deal that
you agreed two years ago might have made a lot of sense
at the time, but now that things have changed in your
business, your supply chain or politically, the deal has
become damaging or unsustainable for you.

Some people will always want to retain an element
of certainty in the deals they agree to and will resist this
approach. Of course, some businesses make their profit
by creating deals that take advantage of an accurate pre-
diction of changes in markets or in their counterparty's
situation. It might not be in their interests to include an
element of flexibility or review in the deal, as they might
want to be locked into a situation that is extremely profitable for them. Or they simply might not want to have to
renegotiate all of their major agreements every few years.

Make sure you explore this before you get to the final
sign-off stages of your deal. Ideally, you should be considering issues like flexibility and contract review terms
way back in the Discover and Establish phases.

Mediation clauses

It may be prudent for you to include mediation clauses in

your final agreement, should a dispute arise. This could be particularly helpful if you are engaged in a longer-term relationship with your counterparty and would like that to continue. The introduction of a third-party mediator can allow you to address contentious or challenging performance or compliance issues without the two sides becoming bogged down in 'he said ..., she said ...' disputes or behaving in ways they might later regret. The inclusion of a mediation or dispute resolution clause should not be seen as a failure or a negative step. Instead it should be viewed as a sensible and pragmatic approach to preserving the health of the future relationship.

Deal or no deal

Up to now we have been talking mainly about scenarios where the outcome is an agreement between the parties. But as we explored right back at the start of the book, sometimes an agreement just cannot be reached and you hit a deadlock. This might come in the form of a reactive stand-off because the parties have clashed with each other, relations have been damaged and there are issues on which people keep getting frustrated and stuck. Or it might be the result of a proactive decision to decide there is no deal to be done. Perhaps this is because the numbers don't add up, the timing isn't right or the parties have decided to pursue other alternatives.

Deadlock and failure

We must remember that our not reaching an agreement (whether because of inability or decision) is not always a negative thing. It's not always a failure. Sometimes it is the logical or prudent answer based on the point we have got to or the simple facts we have in front of us. As we considered in Chapter One, it can be far worse to agree to a deal out of fear of deadlock then it is to cut your losses and walk away. We explored in Common Negotiation Mistake Fifteen (see page 83) that we tend to equate 'yes' with success but that, quite simply, it isn't always true. Your job as a negotiator is to be clear on your definitions of success and failure, to have explored all of the options and to know at what point a deal just isn't viable. At that point, if you need to and are able to, you should consider walking away.

If, however, you feel that you want to try to 'save' the negotiation because you think there is a great deal to be done that you just haven't got to yet, you can try the following tips:

- Take a time-out

- Present new proposals

- Change the parties

- Suggest you reconvene on new terms

- Escalate to a higher authority, such as your boss

- Leave the door open. Even if you think there is no going back and the deal is off, you never know what a few days to cool off might do.

Deals method summary

	Aim of stage	Steps	Tools
Discover	What type of negotiation are you in?	The Five Factor Test; Insight Locker; Mapping the issues; Preconditioning	Variable Mapper
Establish	Understanding each side's priorities	Determining your Takes and Gives; Impact assessment; Finding your breakpoints; Establishing the Negotiation Zone	Issues Analysis Possibilities Plotter
Ask	Planning your proposals	Total Value deals; Opening ambitiously; Opening first	Proposal Planner
Lead	Managing the negotiation as it unfolds	Taking control; Recording the deal; Nothing is agreed until everything is agreed; Holding Pen; Discipline	Deal Sheet
Seal	End of deal summary	Post-deal, pre-paperwork management; Future-proofing the deal; Regular review; Anticipating and dealing with change	

PART THREE

People Negotiate with People

CHAPTER EIGHT

The Balance of Power

Power is one of the most important factors that can influence the outcome of a negotiation. Who has it, who hangs on to it, who uses it and how they use it should be key considerations for anyone involved in planning for an impending negotiation.

We are going to look at some ways to effectively negotiate with someone who has far more power than you, as well as how to negotiate with someone who has far less power than you. Before we do that, we need to explore in a bit more detail the complexities and realities of power and how we can start to think about it a bit differently.

The gift of 'Power Bias'

'In our negotiations the other side has all the power. They are bigger than us, have more money than us and have plenty of other people they could go to in order to get what they need. This means we are losing from the start.'

'Our industry is 100 per cent a buyers' market. Our

customers hold all the cards ... What are we supposed to do?'

These statements give you a picture of the kinds of comments that our clients make to us when we talk to them about the balance of power at the negotiation table. Many people are very quick to assume that their counterparty is the one in the stronger position – and even that this position is far stronger than their own.

Take the example of two concurrent workshops that I ran in Hong Kong. One was for the buying team at a luxury goods retail outlet, and the other was for salespeople at a leather goods company. Both groups would have to negotiate with each other or with similar teams of buyers and salespeople. About a third of the way through the workshops I asked each group of people the question: 'Who has the power in your negotiations?'

The answers? The salespeople said something along the lines of:

'Well it's the buyers. That's obvious. They can just decide not to stock our products in their stores. Then that's it. The ultimate power.'

The buyers at the retail outlet responded to the same question with:

'The sellers. Without a doubt. They can make all sorts of demands and ultimately decide they aren't going to supply to us. Game over.'

The thing is, studies have shown that negotiators have a tendency to approach each deal with the perception that their counterparty has way more than power than they actually do.[13] We gift them power and lumber ourselves with the disadvantage and weakness, often without taking the time to properly assess the reality of the situation. This is because it is far easier for us to focus in on our own situation: why we desperately need to close the deal, the time pressures we are under, the cash flow problems we might have ... These things shape and distort our immediate assumption about where the balance of power lies.

Why is this a gift to our counterparty? The 'Power Bias' can result in us planning for the negotiation far less ambitiously. In some instances, people adopt the mindset of 'I'll be lucky if I even get ...' This kind of attitude immediately limits the outcomes you will be able to achieve. If you go into a negotiation thinking you will be the loser, I would suggest that 99 times out of 100 you will walk away as the loser.

Power doesn't stand still
Power isn't static. It evolves, distorts and moves over time. Your counterparty might have had the upper hand at one stage, but that doesn't mean they will always have it.

Movie rental

Take the example of the fortunes of a well-known high-street retailer. When I was a child, a Friday night would often involve a trip to our local Blockbuster video rental store. My brothers and I would be allowed to go and choose a video and to grab a bag of popcorn or a bottle of Coke. Then on the following Sunday night, we would take the video cassette back to the store and pop it into the video drop-off box, keen to avoid any late fees! Blockbuster was a powerful and well-known brand. With a branch in pretty much every town in a number of countries, it played a key role in the weekend plans of millions of people.

But as technology evolved and personal entertainment systems and tablets became more advanced and affordable, providing customers with an almost-infinite choice of films to download, stream or order by mail, the notion of having to drive to a high-street movie rental store to choose from a limited number of titles became antiquated. Customers abandoned Blockbuster in droves. It couldn't evolve quickly enough. The vast majority of its stores closed. Its power was utterly depleted.

You could also think about politicians, sports teams, entertainers or actors who were extremely talented, powerful and at the top for a while, but then because of a change in personal or external circumstances over time found themselves back at the bottom of the pile. Just because you once had power doesn't mean you will always have it. It moves, it shifts, and it can abandon us or our counterparty completely. So don't consign yourself to forever being the weaker party ... or assume that you will always be the powerful one.

Perceived power vs actual power

Interestingly, it's not always the actual power that makes a difference at the negotiation table. Perceived power can be just as influential in helping you to get the result that you need. We have already said that negotiators have a tendency to gift power to the other side ... well that goes for your counterparty too. They may well have started to think about all the reasons why you are in a stronger position, even if you are not.

So, don't start advertising the fact that you think you're in the weaker position. Think instead about what you might be able to do to build the perception of power. What positioning information can you deploy to help strengthen any perceived power? What statements and language can you use to suggest that you are in a powerful position?

Think powerfully. Act powerfully. It might help strengthen your position, at least in your counterparty's eyes.

The effectiveness of power

The power that you possess is only going to have an impact if you are either willing to utilise it or if your counterparty believes that you will. Power loses its force and becomes benign if no one around you believes that you will use it to get an advantage over them.

A simple example of this would be a CEO who is unwilling to use their power to fire a colleague who routinely underperforms or behaves inappropriately. Or a lecturer who threatens to fail students if they keep turning up late to class, but never does.

After a while, the power starts to fade and dissipate. No one truly believes you are going to do anything with it. And so, the potential benefits and strengths that it could have provided also disappear. So how should we deal with the balance of power?

Assess the balance of power

The first step is always to conduct a rigorous and creative assessment of the balance of power. Don't just automatically assume that you know what the state of play is. Do your research, dig around and look at the world through your counterparty's eyes.

Over the years, a number of academics and researchers have sought to identify the sources of power. One interesting interpretation is that power flows from the pleasure/pain principle. That is, the person who can give out the most pleasure or dispense the most pain is the one who wields the bulk of the power in human interactions.

However a more accessible and useful way to think about the balance of power would be to consider the following four sources of potential power: Personal, Organisational, Information and Moral Power.[14]

Personal Power: This is the power that a person brings to the negotiation. This would include a person's courage, intelligence, appearance, strength, tenacity, memory, logic, confidence, intuition and ability to take risks. We have said already that people negotiate with people, and it follows that when we approach the negotiation table we will be sizing up our counterparty not just in terms of the strength of their organisational position, but also as an individual.

Organisational Power: Given the nature of organisations and the fact that power tends to flow 'top-down', it is of little surprise that a person's position within an organisation will also influence the power dynamics during a negotiation. But we should be careful of assuming that only those with senior executive level titles are the ones with real power. Sometimes it's those people who are well-connected or in highly specialised roles who hold an abundance of power.

Information Power: This is simple. When it comes to negotiation, information is power. The more you know about a situation, the more you can start to accurately assess your position, develop a strategy and plan your response. The internet has made the gathering of relevant information much easier and quicker for negotiators and gives us all no excuse for not researching the facts and background of each case. Information power also comes in the form of being recognised as possessing expertise in a certain area. Being able to credibly assert the title of 'expert' for yourself will greatly impact the power you have to influence others. This has been backed up in studies over the years and is explored further in Chapter Nine on the Psychology of Negotiation.

Moral Power: Moral power refers to situations where negotiators are able to make gains through appealing to a person's sense of morality or fairness. Research suggests that moral appeals tend to elicit the best results when you are able to make a plea to the stronger party to 'put themselves in your shoes'.[15] Of course, moral power won't work in every situation, but it can hold great sway over people who display higher levels of empathy. It should certainly not be written off as wishy-washy.

Factors that can influence the balance of power

In a negotiation there will be a number of factors that will dictate the balance of power between the parties. The following factors can all have a huge impact on the actual balance of power in your negotiation, though it is by no means an exhaustive list. It is essential that you fully consider everything that might influence the strength (or otherwise) of each side:

Alternatives

Have you thought about your alternatives if you are unable to reach a deal in this particular instance? Understanding your 'Best Alternative to Negotiated Agreement' ('BATNA') is essential if you are to understand how much power you really have.[16] In short, the weaker your BATNA the weaker you are; the stronger and more diverse your BATNA the stronger you are. But the same also goes for your counterparty. Make sure you have fully considered what their alternatives might be.

Resources

While this isn't an absolute indicator on its own terms, there is no denying that the party with access to more resources (such as money and manpower) is more likely to be in a stronger position than the party without.

Time

We have already talked about the impact that time can have on the deals we do. In general terms, the party who is under no time pressure is often in a far stronger position than the party who is working to deadlines.

Needing the deal

Put simply, how much do they need this deal? And how much do you need it? What I'm really saying is: how desperate are you? If you know that you really, really need to secure this deal, then your power starts to ebb away slightly, as you know you can't just up and walk away. Of course, your power will also drain away even further if you let your counterparty know that you're desperate.

History

If you have a shared history with your counterparty it can have a huge impact on the power dynamic. The more you know about them, the more rigorously you can plan your strategy and anticipate their proposals to you. But it can also work against you if you have offered them overly generous terms in previous negotiations. The precedent you have set for yourself makes it very hard to move up from that position.

Brand power

Do you give your brand the credit it deserves? My team have carried out a lot of work for the National Health Service in the UK and have observed this in action. Our NHS clients will continuously view themselves as being in the weaker position when negotiating with big suppliers. My response is always:

> 'But you're the NHS! You are one of the most recognised and respected brands in the world, with huge scale, buying power, influence and a huge, loyal fan base. Remember that amazing platform you got at the 2012 Olympics Opening Ceremony? Recognise this power and use it.'

Don't underestimate the prestige and status that your counterparty might attribute to you and hope to benefit from if they align with your brand.

Relationships

Your previous or current relationships can also have a huge bearing on the balance of power. It might be that you enjoy a strong and enduring relationship with your counterparty. This could allow you to manage difficult conversations more effectively and speak more openly. Having a vested interest in each other's success also means they are less likely to try to abuse any power they might have. However, you must also be cautious.

Sometimes having a relationship with your counter-party can diminish your power. This can occur when you limit your actions and aspiration because you don't want to risk damaging the relationship. Maybe you won't open as ambitiously, be as persistent or tenacious, or question them as hard as you would if they were someone you had just met. If our fear of losing a friendship is overriding our efforts to get the best outcome, then suddenly that relationship starts working against us, not for us.

Market conditions

Of course, an obvious factor that impacts the power in a negotiation is the current condition of the market in which each side operates. For example, if you are trading in a market that has just been deregulated to allow for a flush of new and cheaper competitors, this will impact the balance of power for you. If you operate in a market where recent negative headlines and undercover inves-tigations have soured consumer feeling towards you and others like you, then this will also impact the power you have. Take the time to know your counterparty's indus-try and understand their market forces as well as you do your own.

Take the time to consider the four sources of power (Personal, Organisational, Information, Moral) and some of the individual factors that might be impacting your negotiations. Try to do it from a clean and balanced view-point, and leave your Power Bias behind. Instead, take a moment to consider your counterparty's possible Power Bias. Try to see the world through their eyes and consider the factors that, from their perspective, might make them think that it's actually you who has all of the power, not them.

What if they have more power than you?

If after all of this assessment you identify that your counterparty holds a far more powerful position, what do you do? Do you just sit back and hope for the best? Do you approach the negotiation accepting that you are just going to have to get what you can and be grateful? Do you bluff it and try to make them think that you have more power than you really do?

Well, you have a number of options. This kind of situation, where one side has significantly more power than the other is called a 'David and Goliath' scenario. It might seem initially hopeless, but by thinking creatively and playing it smart you can start to level the playing field and get a far better result than you might have hoped for.

Are you ever in the position where you have to negotiate with the 'giant' of your industry? Are there one or two big players that seem to dominate how business is done, set the rules and make all the demands of all those around them? Are you frequently on the receiving end of 'take it or leave it' proposals that are heavily weighted in the giant's favour? Are you concerned that by accepting their proposal you will severely impact your financial position?

It might seem that your only choice, if you are to avoid

being blacklisted or squeezed out of the market, is to take the potentially damaging proposal that they are offering you. It's better to be in the game than to be squeezed out entirely, isn't it?

No. Not always. Sometimes the quality of the offer on the table from the giant in your industry will be so low and so corrosive to your business or personal situation that it is better to walk away.

But what if you can't do that? What if this deal is strategically important to the growth of your business? What if there are going to be wider implications such as job losses or an inability to meet existing obligations?

There is potentially another way. We'll explore a number of different strategies to try to improve your position and walk away with a result that belies your assessment of their supposed strength and your supposed weakness.

Developing the 'elegant solution'

Imagine you have just been presented with that 'take it or leave it' proposal that works heavily in your counterparty's favour and leaves you with very little option or value. What do you do next?

In his book *Good for you, Great for me*, Professor Susskind refers to negotiating with the 900-pound gorilla: a counterparty so strong and powerful that they appear impossible to reason with or overcome. Susskind's approach to overcoming your beast of a counterparty is to try to seek an 'elegant solution' to your predicament. He defines an elegant solution as 'a counterproposal that will create even more value for both sides than what the 900-pound gorilla is trying to impose'.[17] This kind of counterproposal is going to require you to think creatively and be prepared to redefine your initial thinking on what the critical factors of the deal might be.

How do you create this kind of creative counterproposal? The stages to developing an elegant solution for your negotiation are: evolve, understand and grow.

1. **Evolve:** Is there anything that you can do to change your current strategy or approach so that you can meet their demands while strengthening your own position?

2. **Understand:** Further explore the other side's interests: have you really understood what your competitor is seeking to achieve in their marketplace, and not just specifically in the deal here with you? Are they looking to increase market share? Diversify their product offering? Enter into new geographies? Increase their reputation in a restricted market? Target a new customer demographic? Have you fully understood the areas where they might benefit from new thinking?

3. **Grow:** Finally, you should look at other ways to create value for them. Is there any way that you can educate them to see that working more collaboratively with you would be beneficial? What could you offer them to help strengthen their position? How can their interests be advanced by seeing you as a partner

in business rather than just a supplier or a cog in the wheel?

Other strategies to deal with your giant gorilla

Build strategic alliances

Why not try building coalitions with other 'weaker' parties in your negotiations? For example, if your customer has a number of other companies they can purchase from, then you are in a weak position, but so are all of those other companies the customer could go to. Similarly, if your boss has the ability to change your terms and conditions at will, then you are in a weak position, but so are all of your colleagues. The notion of weaker parties forming strategic alliances to lever their power is not a new one. Individuals, companies and countries have been doing it for years.

This is what has led to the emergence of cooperatives and trade unions. It's what makes it harder for giants to pit one weaker party against another. This serves to remove the giant's BATNA, making their position that much less powerful than it was when you were all working against each other, rather than with each other.

Consider alternative sources of power

People will traditionally assume that the sources of power that matter most in a negotiation are size, money and resources. However, if upon analysing these factors it is clear that your counterparty is in the stronger position, explore whether you might have any other, less obvious tools at your disposal. In the following example,

Greenpeace was by far the weaker party when it came to the three traditional power factors just mentioned. But it had another, alternative source of power: its loyal and passionate supporters, and it was able to use this to tip the balance of power completely into its favour.

Greenpeace and Nestlé palm oil dispute

In 2010, global consumer giant Nestlé was listed in a report by Greenpeace as sourcing palm oil for its products from a supplier that was damaging the natural habitat of a number of endangered species including the orang-utan.[18] Greenpeace began a campaign to encourage Nestlé to change its buying practices. Of course, when you compare Greenpeace and Nestlé, the latter is far larger and wealthier than the former. You might assume that Nestlé could have brushed off the attentions of Greenpeace or sued them into submission.

However, the balance of power between the two was tipped due to Greenpeace's 'alternative power source', its hundreds of thousands of loyal and passionate supporters. Greenpeace launched a social media onslaught at Nestlé, and its supporters followed suit. Nestlé was bombarded with over 200,000 emails, hundreds of phone calls and mass criticism on its Facebook and Twitter feeds. Criticism of Nestlé grew, demands for global boycotts from consumers intensified, and the brand began to be tarnished. After only ten weeks, Nestlé announced it would change palm oil suppliers. A major victory for

Greenpeace, the smaller and at first glance, seemingly weaker party.

This kind of approach has been used on numerous occasions by members of the public who harness social media power to get their message across and to strengthen their bargaining position. Take the examples of consumers who shame their utilities or mobile phone provider's poor customer service on Twitter, generating thousands of retweets and extracting apologies and compensation from their giant in the process. Or the millions of people who have used online petition and campaigning sites such as change.org to take on oppression and bullying or simply to challenge perceived unfair practices or policies. Victories on the change.org site have included changes to government practice, changes in the process of social housing allocation and even the release of a prisoner from an Iranian jail.[19] These are all examples of how people have looked for alternative sources of power to fight back against their giant who, on paper, is far stronger than them.

Appeal to their better nature
If you have just received an excessive demand from your powerful counterparty in relation to pricing, it can be tempting to see them as a greedy, money-obsessed giant of a company that cares only about bottom line. Now in some circumstances, that might be the case. But in others, you might be able to take advantage of the fact

that people negotiate with people and appeal to someone's better nature to encourage them to rethink their proposal. You can do this on two levels.

First, you could seek to appeal to the wider aspirations of the company as a whole. Try to find out how the company measures success and what constitutes a threat or a headache. For example, you might seek to address:

- **Quality:** *'I can see that price is important to you, and I'm sure there are others out there who are offering to deliver this service more cheaply, but I can guarantee that at prices lower than ours, quality is going to be compromised. You know we deliver a service with consistently high levels of quality. Is a continuation of quality to your consumers important to you?'*

- **Flexibility:** *'We have always tried to work in partnership with you and have been flexible if a problem has arisen on your side. A new supplier might not have the insight or resources to be as flexible as we have been. Is this ability to adapt to the needs of your business something that you value?'*

- **Expertise:** *'We have always recognised that you admire and rely on our principal partner on this project. They have developed a real insight into your business and can provide tailored advice as a result. Is maintaining this skilled level of resource important to the smooth operation of your business?'*

You could also try the second option, which is to appeal to someone's personal sense of fairness or justice. Earlier I warned against making all of your decisions in a negotiation based on fairness, but the fact is that many of us are heavily swayed by and guided by it as a principle or aspiration. This means that there is a chance your counterparty may also be open to persuasion on the basis of these principles.

Of course, you need to think strategically about who you appeal to. The commission-driven middle manager who has the mandate to get the best deal at all costs is probably not the right person, but their boss, or their boss's boss, who has an eye on the bigger picture and the possible financial, operational and reputational implications of a deal, might well be.

Play by the rules

The old story of how the notorious gangster Al Capone ended up snared on tax evasion charges is a well-known example of how even the most powerful people need to play by (at least some of) the rules. When it comes to a power imbalance, you might want to consider looking at the rules, regulations and governance around the issue you are negotiating. Is your counterparty doing things by the book? Are they keeping their house in order? Have they ticked every box? Have they developed their proposal to you based on an inaccurate set of facts or a misunderstanding of the relevant rules?

If you discover that they are cutting corners (intentionally or otherwise), you have two possible options:

you can use their non-compliance as a lever to increase your power, or you can position yourself as someone who can assist them in addressing the issue. The option you choose will probably be driven by the relationship you have, or wish to have, with them, but in either situation your power may well increase if you are able to show that their practices make them vulnerable.

If you are the giant gorilla?

What about if you're the one with all the power? Tread carefully. Think about how you exercise your power. Do not think that this means you are invincible.

You might well choose to use your power to strong-arm your counterparty to agree to a deal that works very much in your favour but you will run the risk of that deal becoming vulnerable to being undermined, pulled apart, poorly delivered or breached altogether if there is no real incentive for your counterparty to perform. There is certainly precedent to suggest that oppressive or enforced agreements are inherently unstable.[20]

It can be very easy to become drunk on power. But don't abuse it. Don't run your counterparty into the ground or penalise them unnecessarily. If you deprive them of everything they've got, it makes it far easier for them to walk away, which in turn might leave you very vulnerable indeed.

CHAPTER NINE

The Psychology of Negotiation

As part of my job I regularly speak at conferences and seminars around the world on the topic of effective negotiation. I provide tips, tools and advice to men and women across different continents, in different industries, with differing levels of experience. Whether I am addressing a handful of people or a conference room of hundreds I will always carry out a little exercise to help people understand the magic ingredient of negotiation.

I ask the people in the audience to find a partner and identify who will be a buyer and who will be a seller. I give each couple a pack containing a case study. In the case study there is a set of instructions for the buyer and another for the seller. I advise the audience that they will have four minutes to read the brief, followed by five minutes to negotiate a deal.

The brief is very simple. It concerns the possible acquisition of an antique in a situation where both the buyer and the seller are keen to do a deal. It is a one-off transaction where the key issue to be negotiated is price. Based on the individual briefs, it is made clear that the seller cannot accept any lower than £12,000 and the buyer cannot pay anything higher then £16,000. Using some simple facts in the brief, each party can have a pretty good guess as to what their counterparty's breakpoint might be.

At the end of the exercise, after I have called time, I ask the audience to report back. I ask for a show of hands as to who reached a deal, and a show of hands as to who didn't. I then ask the room to put their hands in the air if they finished in the region of each of the following points. I start by shouting out: 'Who got around £12,000?' I then ask the same question in £500 increments all the way up to £16,000.

Hands in the audience all go up at different times. There is no one point at which every hand in the room shoots up. Some finish at £12,000, some at £16,000 and others finish at widely varying points between that range. Some won't reach a deal at all.

So why do I do the exercise? I don't ask each couple to explain their negotiation and why they each finished where they did. I am far more interested in the simple fact that different couples get different outcomes and that there is no one point of consensus. This is despite the fact that everyone in the audience had:

- The same set of facts for each buyer and each seller
- The same instructions from me

- The same amount of time
- The same location.

This reveals a key lesson you should take away from reading this book: *the most important ingredient in negotiation is the people.*

Why do the couples in the audience all finish at different points in the Negotiation Zone? It's quite simply because people are people, and all people are different. Negotiation is not just about the numbers, regulations, facts or the strength of an individual case or corporate position. Negotiation is about how people react and respond to each other; how we perceive each other, test each other, read each other and view each other; how far we think we can push someone and how far we are willing to be pushed; our feelings, emotions, fears and ambitions; our interpretation of success and our definition of failure; and a whole host of other very individual factors that will change from person to person.

This is why some people can be given a seemingly hopeless case on the facts but walk away with an amazing outcome, and why others can be given a relative 'walk in the park' where the facts all seem to work in their favour but end up with a poor result. How human beings interact with each other can make all the difference in the deals we do.

In this chapter, we are going to explore some of the fascinating elements of human behaviour and psychology that influence the negotiations that we do every day in both our personal and professional lives.

Negotiation theory and the reality of people

For a number of years, a lot of negotiation theory was very driven by economics, mathematics and the analysis of decision-making. I'm sure you will have heard of game theory (or at least seen the film *A Beautiful Mind* starring Russell Crowe, based on the life of John Nash, a Nobel Laureate and leading expert in the field of the analysis of games and decision-making). Game theory can be described as the mathematical study of decision-making, of conflict and strategy in social situations, and it helps explain how we interact in key decision-making processes. It is seen as one of the fundamental pillars in negotiation theory.

Game theory focuses on problems and simulations where the protagonists in a dispute are all logical and each side knows and fully understands the rules of the game. Immediately, therefore, we have a problem in applying game theory to real-life negotiations. The problem is that in many everyday disputes and negotiations the people involved don't necessarily fully understand the rules or the behaviours of the other side, and they don't follow particularly logical strategies. In short, the fact that we are regular people gets in the way. The realities of how we make decisions and interact with others can sometimes directly contradict that which is expected of us in classic economic approaches such as game theory.

THE PSYCHOLOGY OF NEGOTIATION 189

'Dumber, nicer and weaker': predicting behaviour

The academics Herbert Simon and Richard Thaler explored a phenomenon throughout the 1980s and 90s: they looked at the distinction between *Homo Economicus* and *Homo Psychologicus*, the distinction between how human beings make decisions and conduct themselves based on either the clean rationality of economics or the messy reality of psychology.[21] Simon's view was that that generally people are 'dumber, nicer and weaker' than classical economic theory predicts.[22]

I would assert that game theory and other economic models of how people approach decision-making, and therefore interactions such as negotiations, just don't reflect the complexities and irregularities of human behaviour. As human beings we can be guided by ambition, fear, passion, worry, hope, apprehension and excitement, and sometimes we will make decisions that are inconsistent, inefficient or based on irrelevant information. Despite this, there are some predictable patterns in how humans behave when making decisions that can start to be understood, pre-empted and used to inform and improve our performance during our negotiations.

Our predictable irrationality

We will talk in Chapter Ten about how to overcome perceived irrationality from your counterparty when you are going through the negotiation process. Well, it's not just our counterparty and their irrationality that we need to be worried about. It turns out there are a whole host of things that negotiators are almost systematically pre-programmed to do or to be affected by. These things appear in no way to be supported by rationality, logic or optimality.

If you're happy and you know it

Research has shown that our emotions can disproportionately affect the decisions we make at the negotiation table. Positive moods tend to increase a negotiator's tendency to adopt a cooperative stance and to enhance their ability to find integrative gains. In direct contrast to this, angry negotiators are less capable at judging their counterparty's interests, and achieve lower joint gains.[23] Make sure you check the temperature of your emotions before you take your seat at the negotiation table – and check those of your counterparty!

Putting on the blinkers

Bounded awareness[24] is the phenomenon by which individuals do not 'see' or use certain pieces of readily accessible and perceivable information during the decision-making process while seeing and using other equally accessible and perceivable information. In short, our brains choose to see some things and to disregard others, even when the information is of comparative usefulness and value. This phenomenon is heightened when we have been directed to focus on another task. In these instances, we tend to suffer even more from missing the bleeding obvious and ignore relevant information that is readily available and right under our nose.

This can present a real danger area in negotiations, especially if our counterparty has attempted to precondition us to consider particular issues as important (those more favourable to them) at the expense of others (those which might make them vulnerable). Our tendency to focus on the directed task rather than to fully assess and absorb the other information staring us in the face could result in us missing huge opportunities or disregarding aspects of the deal that could tip the balance of power in our favour.

Positive framing

A number of studies in the 1990s showed that negotiators are highly likely to be more concessionary in a negotiation that is positively framed than one that is negatively framed.[25] Take this example: researchers presented people with two types of meat; one was labelled '99 per cent fat-free' and the other was labelled '1 per cent fat'. Respondents were asked to choose which meat was healthier. The participants labelled the first option as being far healthier, even though both are, of course, identical. Even when the labels were changed to '98 per cent fat-free' and '1 per cent fat', the group still ranked the first option as healthier, despite its higher fat content. The difference was all in the phrasing and the way the options were framed to the respondents.

According to Amos Tversky and Daniel Kahneman, whether people avoid or embrace risk depends on how the decision is framed.[26] Almost any decision can be framed as a gain or loss relative to a specific point of reference. The key is to understand what your counter-party considers to be a gain or a loss, what their success and failure criteria are. Clever negotiators should think about how to frame their proposals to the other side by carefully selecting what those points of reference are and incorporating them into the negotiation.

Subsequent research into this issue discovered that in a controlled study where participants were given identical financial briefs but differing instructions as to whether to 'cut their losses' or 'maximise their gains' in a negotiation, those who were told to cut their losses made fewer concessions and behaved in a riskier fashion than those told to focus on their gains.[27]

Ideally, in a negotiation you should aim for your counterparty to be in a 'gain' frame. This will increase the chances of them accepting your proposal. Of course, you still need to be aware that while you can frame, you can also *be* framed, so watch out!

Fixed Pie Bias

The Fixed Pie Bias is the natural inclination that nego-tiators have to view the interaction as involving a 'fixed pie' to be sliced up and distributed between the parties, rather than as an interaction that could include mutually beneficial trade-offs and a 'growing of the pie' in order to unlock and distribute more value. Research over a fifteen-year period showed that negotiators do indeed tend to assume the negotiation is one involving only a fixed amount of value.[28]

To counter this effect, it would be worth checking

your assumptions and forcing yourself to think creatively as to what issues could be traded and what value
could be explored (over and above the obvious) in your
forthcoming deal.

The influence of influence

At the start of this chapter, I pointed out that negotiation
is a lot more than just understanding theory and process
and having the right numbers and projections in front of
you. Negotiation is also about how people interact with
each other. Our capacity to influence other people will
have a huge impact on the deals that we do. Whether we
can persuade someone to agree to a proposal, change
their position or amend previously held beliefs will go a
long way to helping us get the outcome that we need at
the negotiation table.

Some practitioners believe that the ability to persuade others has nothing to do with how successfully we
negotiate. That if you don't have the right facts and information or your case isn't strong enough, no matter what
you do to try to influence others, or persuade them to
agree to your course of action, you will not get the result
you need.

I could not disagree more. We would be very naïve
to think that we will get the best results by only focusing on the facts and the numbers. Your counterparty is
human, just like you. Your ability to read, understand and
influence that human is going to have a bearing on that
interaction.

Similarly, you would be foolish to approach a

negotiation without having done your research and having all of the relevant information at your fingertips. A strategy of relying on your charm, wit and ability to build rapport would be incredibly dangerous.

The ability to influence others and to persuade them to agree to things is an integral part of the process of negotiation. But so is having the right facts, figures and projections at your disposal. You can't just rely on having one of the two elements of the equation. Your best results are going to come from mastering both parts of the puzzle.

The influencing laws – the science bit

For over 60 years, researchers have been studying what influences us to agree with or concede to others. It seems that there is a science to how we are persuaded rather than just being affected by a blend of charm and wit!

In the age of information overload, it is impossible for our brains to process absolutely every piece of relevant information at our fingertips when we are presented with a decision. Indeed, sometimes we take only moments to make a decision, such as whether or not to cross the road or to smile at a stranger. As a result, our brains have developed a number of shortcuts to assist us in the process. Dr Robert Cialdini is one of the experts at the forefront of this area of study, and his book *Influence: The psychology of persuasion* presents six universal shortcuts or 'laws' that will impact our decision-making: Reciprocity, Scarcity, Authority, Consistency, Liking and Consensus.

Understanding these six laws is essential for any negotiator, not only so that you can utilise them in your deals to try to secure preferential outcomes but also so you can start to assess whether the laws are something that your counterparty has been using to try to persuade you to make certain choices.

I have adapted Cialdini's laws to create a simple persuasion toolkit for the negotiation table. For each of the laws, you will find Negotiation Tips that illustrate ways you can use this insight to improve your negotiation outcomes, both simply and ethically. I should state clearly that I am not advocating you use these laws in a deceptive or unethical manner.

1. The law of Reciprocity: the obligation to give something back if you have received something from others.

This plays on the idea of Take and Give that we explored in Chapter Two. Research shows that we are highly influenced by the act of someone giving something to us. In one study, which took place in a restaurant, when a waiter gave the customer a mint along with the bill, their tip increased by an average of 3 per cent. Leaving two mints increased the tip customers gave by 14 per cent. But the biggest indicator of how much they received in return for giving was dictated by *how* waiters 'made the Give'. When the waiter left one mint, walked away but then turned and provided a second mint, saying 'but for you nice people, here's another', the tip increased by 23 per cent.[29] In short, the Give should be personalised and above and beyond traditional expectations.

Negotiation Tip: Think about what you can give your counterparty, not just in the negotiation, but in any interactions you might have beforehand. If you are able to give them something, even something small like a coffee or a book you have recommended, it will precondition them to be in a giving mindset towards you. Similarly, if you are looking to gain more information from them, try giving them some information first in order to encourage reciprocal behaviour.

2. The law of Scarcity: people want things that are in short supply. An opportunity seems more valuable to us when its availability is limited.

This explains the success of limited edition goods such as cars, shoes, handbags and artwork. If something is 'exclusive and time-limited' we are drawn to it, as it makes us feel that we are in a special minority or set apart from everyone else around us. This is why the limited number tactic is so frequently used by retailers. The fear of potential loss is a huge factor in the human decision-making process and can be used to influence the outcomes in your negotiations.

Negotiation Tip: Consider how you position your product, service or position when you are planning your negotiation. If you can evidence that what you have to offer is rare or restricted in number, or that the offer will only be able to stand for a limited amount of time, then your counterparty's scarcity fears might kick in, encouraging them to want what you have in a way that perhaps they didn't before. Similarly, if you are describing your proposition to your counterparty, you might want to consider not only highlighting the benefits they will gain, why it is unique, but also what they stand to lose if they don't get their hands on it.

3. The law of Authority: we are naturally inclined to follow the lead of credible and knowledgeable experts.

A study at a real-estate letting agency found that they experienced a 20 per cent rise in appointments and a 15 per cent increase in signed contracts when receptionists explicitly mentioned industry credentials before introducing a potential customer to a colleague.[30] The visibility of our expertise or standing will also help persuade others to behave in a certain way. A study showed that people were more likely to agree to a stranger's request for change to pay a parking meter if the stranger was dressed in a professional uniform of some kind. Similarly, physiotherapists reported an increase in client compliance with prescribed exercise programmes if they had copies of diplomas and degrees displayed on the wall behind them at the point of making their request.

Negotiation Tip: Try thinking about ways that you can educate your counterparty as to your industry credentials, perhaps displaying qualifications in an office or a summary of recognised achievements in an information pack or on your website. You should also think about including a visible authority or recognised industry expert in a negotiating team or taking them along to any pre-deal exploratory meetings.

4. The law of Consistency: people prefer to be consistent with things that they have previously said or done. Once we have committed to something, we tend to stick to it.

This is why people stay loyal to brands that might be more expensive, or why they tend to donate to the same charities again and again. It seems that once we take a stand and commit to something, we will make future choices to remain consistent with our initial decision. In addition to this, people are not only driven to *be* consistent, but are also driven to *appear to be* consistent. This is because, socially, consistency is a desirable personality trait. It is seen as trustworthy, decisive and stable. Inconsistency, on the other hand, is commonly viewed as a negative trait and is viewed as deceptive, indecisive and unstable.

Negotiation Tip: Think about how you can encourage your counterparty to agree to something small that works in your favour. Perhaps if negotiating with a customer you might get them to agree on one occasion to be marginally flexible on payment terms. The next time you negotiate with them on this point, you could request slightly more preferential changes on payment terms. Their desire to appear consistent may mean that they agree to this more readily than if this were the first time you had made such a request.

5. The law of Liking: we prefer to say 'yes' to people that we like.

The evidence tells us that three elements will

encourage someone to like us: similarity, receiving compliments and a willingness to cooperate. In a study of simulated negotiations between MBA students, some were told to adopt a 'time is money' approach and get straight down to business.[31] In this group, 55 per cent of people were able to get to agreement. Of the second group, who were told to spend some time before the negotiation exchanging personal information and identifying a similarity, 90 per cent were able to reach agreements that were, on average, 18 per cent more profitable for each side. Another study found that marchers at a political rally were more likely to sign a petition if the person making the request was dressed like them.[32]

Negotiation Tip: Look for ways before the negotiation to build rapport with your counterparty. Research where they went to school, what hobbies they have, whether they have kids … anything that could allow you to identify an area of similarity. You could also take cues from how they dress and try to dress similarly in style or tone. You could also look for opportunities to make compliments about them – just make sure they are genuine and don't make you look like you are deliberately trying to butter them up! In short, look for areas of common ground, aspects of their approach or behaviour that you admire, and then share that with them.

6. The law of Consensus: when in doubt, people will look to the actions of others to shape the choices they make, particularly of others similar to themselves. This is also referred to as 'social proofing' or the 'if everyone else is doing it ...' syndrome.

Negotiation Tip: Look for ways that you can show your counterparty how popular your product or service is. Share testimonials, let them know how many of their competitors or peers are working with you, cite mentions you have had in the press, show information on the levels of previous sales. Share anything that shows just how many other people have made the (sensible and enlightened!) decision to engage with you. If you are already engaged with your counterparty in an existing relationship and are looking to seek their agreement on a change of existing terms (perhaps you are looking to encourage all customers to move to a different service package), you might try letting them know how many of their competitors have already made the switch.

Other ways to get people to agree with you

Give a reason: Research by Harvard psychologist Ellen Langer showed that we are more likely to grant someone a favour if they give us a reason for doing so.[33] It seems people just like to have reasons for what they are doing. In her experiment involving a request to jump the queue at a photocopying machine, she found that if a reason was given for the request ('I have to make five copies. Can I jump the line because I am in a rush?'), the request was granted 94 per cent of the time. Whereas if the request was made without any reason ('I have to make five copies. Can I jump the line?'), it only generated a positive response 60 per cent of the time.

At first glance, it seems that the key factor in securing compliance is the use of the explanation as to why you need to queue jump. But it became clear that any explanation, whether it was valid or not, was just as effective. When the request changed to 'Can I jump the line because I have to make five copies?' the compliance rose again to 93 per cent. The key word appears to be 'because'.

Negotiation Tip: Think about how you can phrase requests for things from your counterparty. Imagine you want to postpone a meeting. Rather than saying 'I need to move the meeting. Can we reschedule to Thursday?', instead try 'I need to move the meeting because I won't be available. Can we reschedule to Thursday?' My caveat with this advice is to make sure your 'because' doesn't expose a weakness in your negotiating position, such as a punishing time pressure or a level of desperation on your part. The type of negotiation you are in should influence how this tip is used.

Encourage positive behaviours: The reinforcement principle is the way in which we can positively reward the behaviours we want to see in others in order to encourage them to exhibit more of the same.

Professor Leigh Thompson, in her book *The Truth about Negotiations,* refers to a group of students who tested the reinforcement principle on their lecturer. Whenever the lecturer walked to the right side of the classroom, they would all nod encouragingly, smile and sit forward in their seats. When the lecturer went to the left side they would slump, look away and disengage. It's not surprising that as a result the lecturer spent the bulk of his time in the right side of the room. Think also of how parents encourage babies and toddlers to develop new skills. When a child successfully feeds themselves, takes their first steps, practises counting or tidies up their mess, parents respond with smiles, nods, claps and cries of 'well done'!

Negotiation Tip: The reinforcement principle could be a very valuable tool in negotiation to allow you to encourage behaviours that work in your favour. Ideally, you would want to encourage your counterparty to exhibit behaviours that help to unlock value and maximise the potential of the deal, such as sharing information or making concessions. Behaviour rewards could be very subtle, such as a smile or a nod, or they could be a phrase such as 'I appreciate that', 'This is great' or 'Fantastic idea'.

The image we project to others

In the DEALS chapter of this book, we explored that when you are in a negotiation it is important to think about all of the messaging that you might be giving to others, rather than just the ones you are conscious of giving.

It's no secret that when we are stressed, anxious, nervous or under pressure we will start to do things that we wouldn't normally dream of doing and utter things we wouldn't normally say. And while we will be aware of some of them – e.g. thinking 'what on earth did I just say that for?' – we won't be aware of others at all – e.g. continuously twitching our foot or pulling on our hair.

We've discussed already that people negotiate with people, and as a result of this, one of the ways we seek to understand our counterparty is to read the messages that they are giving out to us. But people don't just read the conscious messages given, they also look for and interpret unconscious messages that might signal more closely how we feel or what we really mean.

In this section we are going to look at the impact of our body language and of the words and phrases we use during a negotiation. We'll also look at how to be more in control of the messages and image that we project to others. This isn't intended to be a complete or in-depth analysis of the science of communication, rather an overview of some key points that you can use to start making small but significant improvements.

Human beings have been communicating through signs and body language far longer than we have through formal spoken language. Indeed when we go to a country where we don't speak the local language we will rely on poses and gesturing to get our message across. Similarly, before children learn to talk they communicate through facial expressions and physical displays.

Body language is an essential tool for helping us to understand how someone feels, whether they are being truthful, if they like us and what they might do next. Professor Albert Mehrabian's famous studies into interpreting people's feelings and attitudes found that there are three major components of how we assess communications:

- What is said
- How it is said
- The accompanying body language.[34]

What is interesting about the findings of his research is that when we are attempting to understand how someone thinks and feels, if we perceive there to be a mismatch between a person's body language and what they are saying (this is known as an 'incongruence') it is the body language that we will instinctively trust as the deciding factor.

Body language plays a crucial role in understanding, interpreting and categorising the actions, behaviours and feelings of others. We should not underestimate the strength of the messages we give out through our gestures, stance and expressions, and we certainly shouldn't underestimate the insight it can give us into our counterparty.

Everyone will exhibit different 'tells' or cues (physical demonstrations of your emotional state) at different times. You might have a tendency to excessively click your pen when nervous or to pull on the end of your nose when experiencing pressure, stress or anxiety. Just because your counterparty isn't exhibiting those specific tells doesn't mean that they aren't experiencing those emotions or that they aren't exhibiting different tells of their own.

Body language cues to watch out for

In our workshops we often film the attendees in a simulated high-pressure negotiation. The attendees demonstrate a number of cues that could indicate stress or a lack of confidence, such as:

- Folding the arms across the body
- Fidgeting
- Shifting or swinging in their seat
- Biting their lower lip
- Half smiles
- Excessive blinking
- Touching their face
- Tapping their feet
- Persistent short coughs
- Chewing on a pen
- Excessive gesticulation
- Avoiding eye contact
- Making themselves physically smaller
- Rapid breathing.

As the philosopher Immanuel Kant wrote: 'The hands are the visible part of the brain.' If you or your counterparty is feeling stressed or lacking in confidence, it might show in certain tells. First and most importantly you should identify your own body language tells. The sooner you are aware of the physical signals you are giving out and can understand how they might look to others, the better prepared you are to control them. If you are aware of demonstrating any of the above stress cues, focus on those behaviours and work to replace them with calmer, more controlled gestures. Try these tips to help you feel, and appear, more confident and in control:

- Breathe – deeply and slowly

- Keep a glass of water close by to prevent coughing and dry mouth

- Stand or sit tall and keen your chin up

- Make a point of checking your shoulders haven't hunched up towards your ears and drop them downwards

- Sit or stand solidly to feel more grounded – keep both feet planted on the floor

- Hold on to the arms of your chair to prevent fidgeting and shifting around

- Keep your hands still – try lacing your fingers together or placing them in your lap. Avoid messing with a pen

- If you must gesticulate, try to use defined, controlled and slower movements

- Rather than direct eye contact, look at the space just between the other person's eyebrows when addressing them – it can be less intense and is not obvious

- Lean in, look interested

- Find an alternative fidget – something that allows you to release your tension without being seen. An example of this is to consciously wriggle your toes in your shoes when feeling stressed, anxious or unsure. It's a great release but no one knows that you are doing it.

> ### What is the optimum angle at which to stand for persuasiveness?
>
> According to Iain Morley QC, author of the book *The Devil's Advocate*, the answer is 84.5 degrees. Ninety degrees is too upright and makes you look rigid and on edge. This angle makes you appear more relaxed but also connected and engaged by leaning forward!

Now that we've explored some of the things to watch out for in others (and to control in yourself), there's one caveat. While many of these tells and signals can be used as indicators as to what someone might really be thinking or feeling, they are by no means foolproof. The fact that someone is tapping their foot doesn't necessarily make them a liar, just as a few 'ums' and 'ers' in a sentence doesn't always mean they have no idea what they are talking about.

Try to think of other people's tells and signals as prompts for further consideration and exploration. You should apply the three Cs as a guide:

1. **Clusters:** A single indictor on its own isn't enough. Someone averting their eyes mid-sentence doesn't

necessarily mean they are misleading you. But if you can triangulate your observation with a couple of other indicators, such as fidgeting or a frantic tapping of the foot, then you should start to think about what is really going on.

2. **Context:** We must be mindful of the fact that for some people, certain phrases or movements are simply habits picked up over the years and actually mean very little. For example, many people routinely use the phrase 'to be honest' in conversation with others as little more than a way to couch a statement, rather than as an attempt to mislead, e.g. 'I'm not sure what the weather will be like tomorrow to be honest.' (We'll come back to padding phrases like 'to be honest' on page 214.) If you know the person you are negotiating with or have had the chance to observe them before the negotiation table and you notice that they routinely say 'to be honest', you could chalk it up to being little more than a habit rather than a warning flag during the negotiation. If, however, they don't routinely say that phrase but then right when you start to talk about price in the negotiation they say 'I can't go any higher than that to be honest', you should start to take an interest.

3. **Change:** A sudden or unexpected change in your counterparty's body language or verbal communication is often a solid indicator that there is something you need to probe, challenge or explore further.

Hear it, bank it, test it

Now that you can detect them, what you should do if you spot any of the telltale signs or giveaways in your counterparty's body language or verbal communication? I certainly do not advocate shouting:

> *'Aha! You just continuously tapped your foot and coughed nervously! You must be lying!'*

Or pointing your finger and saying:

> *'I knew it! Caught in the act. You just said "to be honest with you" which means that certainly is NOT your best offer!'*

Can I suggest that this will probably cause a bit of friction for the rest of the negotiation? A far better strategy is to hear it, bank it and test it.

Because body language and spoken phrases are only indictors of the truth and not absolutes, we would be wise to explore our assumptions thoroughly before acting upon them, especially if we are going to have to work with our counterparty post-deal. This is where the 'hear it, bank it and test it' method comes in. It allows you to:

- Hear or see the indicator that causes you concern;

- Bank it in your memory; and then

- Test it by using effective investigative questioning to pick apart the validity of what you have just been told.

You don't have long to nail it

Our body language, presence and physical appearance is often the first thing that we are judged on when we meet a stranger.

It has also been suggested that when we meet someone for the first time, we make eleven judgements about that person in the first seven seconds of the interaction, including their level of education, level of wealth, how honest they are, political preference, social desirability and level of sophistication. Given that you can't get that many words out in seven seconds, we can assume that a lot of this is therefore guided by what they can see of us physically.

But it doesn't end there. In subsequent research in 2006, psychologists discovered that it actually takes just one tenth of a second for us to make a multi-faceted judgement about a person.[35]

So it's essential that you work on your posture, expressions, presence and movements. Think about what you want your counterparty's assessment of you to be and then identify ways for your body language to project that message. As the old saying goes: 'You don't get a second chance to make a first impression.'

The things we say and what they mean

Another way for people to gain understanding as to how someone is really feeling or what they really mean is to listen to the words and phrases they use. This can give you real insight into how honest they might be, whether or not they can still move further, and how confident, stressed or anxious they are feeling.

Mean what you say and say what you mean

In order to be perceived as a confident individual who is consistent and clear, you need to think very carefully about whether the words you use confirm or contradict what it is you think you are saying.

A common mistake that people make is to use language that sends an underlying message of 'I don't really mean what I say'. By subconsciously using words and phrases that expose their underlying weaknesses, ability to move or uncertainty as to their position, they give their counterparty areas where they might be able to push harder, dig deeper and expose vulnerabilities. An example of this would be the way that someone phrases their proposal to you. Imagine you are negotiating with the seller of a painting and they say:

'I'm looking for something in the region of around about £100.'

How does that proposal come across to you? Does it sound firm? Or does it sound moveable? Confident or cautious? You can break the proposal up to pick apart its true meaning.

What you hear	How you interpret it
I'm looking for …	*… but I don't hope to get it.*
Something in the region of …	*I feel uncomfortable with this, so I'm letting you know this is just a suggestion.*
Around about £100	*… but if you offer me £80, or even £70, I would take it in a shot.*

The problem is that the proposal just isn't strong or definitive enough. It's too vague, wishy-washy and cautious. The unwillingness to state a clear figure suggests this person is trying their luck, feels uncomfortable about their proposal and would really accept far less. Because the person feels uncomfortable or cheeky about asking for this price, they pad out the sentence, trying to hide or detract from the price they are about to request.

Why does this matter? Because people notice. They hear the uncertainty in the proposal. They hear the discomfort in the phrases used. And they will start to use it to their advantage. A clever negotiator knows that their proposals need to be firm and concise, leaving no room for doubt, uncertainty or challenge.

One of the things I have observed in countless negotiations is that when somebody really means something, their words and phrases become far more succinct, sharp and specific:

'The price is £100.'

Now that's someone who says what they mean and means what they say. By planning your proposals in advance (see the DEALS chapter for advice on this), you can ensure that the phrases and words you use send a clear and defined message. Tell them what your proposal is, don't apologetically ramble your way to the request.

Volume and depth

We also need to think about the tone and depth of our voice when communicating with our counterparty. Research has shown that people associate power and influence with deeper voices. High-pitched or fragile-sounding voices are not perceived to convey a sense of authority and experience. You can combine this with the power of volume. People who present their proposals at a volume that's hard to hear aren't perceived as inspiring, impactful or influential in the way that someone who speaks up and commands the room will be perceived.

A variable tone is also preferable to talking in monotone. People respond well to those who can convey passion, enthusiasm or certainty through the sound of their voice. People who speak with no intonations come across as uninspiring or as though they are simply reading from a script.

The Australian

In addition to watching out for volume and tone, we need to watch out for something often referred to as 'the Australian'. This is our tendency to deliver statements or proposals in such a way that our tone of voice inflects upwards at the end of the sentence. The name comes from the fact that this intonation occurs quite readily in the Australian accent. However, for those of us not from Down Under, it can imply that we are asking a question rather than making a statement, thus making us look unsure or like we are seeking permission from the other party rather than advising them as to the facts.

Get rid of the fillers and padding

When we are thinking about how to respond or about what we had planned to say next, we tend to fill the thinking time with fillers. Fillers are short sounds or words that fill in the gap to make it look like we haven't actually stopped talking and aren't desperately trying to work out our next move. Except, of course, they do the complete opposite, making us sound unprepared, uncertain and nervous. Fillers include 'um', 'er', 'y'know' and 'kind of like'.

The final thing to look out for are phrases such as: *'To be honest with you'* or *'To tell you the truth'*.

Now, I'm not asserting that every time someone comes out with a phrase like this they are lying to you. But I do think we should view them as a warning that something your counterparty has just said sits uncomfortably with them, even if just on a subconscious level. I call these 'padding phrases'. We use them to make ourselves feel better about the fact that we might have just bent the truth, withheld information or proposed a 'best price' that is in fact nothing like our best. They act as a pad or a level of insulation between us and the inaccurate statement we have just made.

Tips for persuasive speech

Let's recap on how to mean what you say and say what you mean, focusing on both the words you use and the way in which you speak:

- Breathe deeply and slowly

- Speak from your belly, rather than from your throat

- Count to three in your head before you answer a question

- Slow down the speed of your responses and try pausing for a moment between sentences and before making key points

- Practise deepening the tone of your voice (trust me, it can be done!)

- Keep it simple and succinct

- Plan your proposals in advance

- Eradicate phrases and words that suggest you are moveable

- Think about varying the tone of your voice

- Avoid using fillers

- Don't be afraid of silence – it can be a very powerful way of provoking a response from your counterparty.

You can hear a lot when you listen

Remember that you need to watch out for cues in both yourself and your counterparty. The ability to observe all of the spoken word cues relies greatly on your ability to properly *listen* to your counterparty.

Listening is a very underrated skill and something that many of us are actually not that great at. We often confuse simply not talking over someone as listening to them. But listening effectively doesn't just require you to stop what you are saying, it also requires you to commit to engaging with what your counterparty is saying.

When I attended Bar School I remember being given this piece of advice about listening:

> *Listen not just to what's being said, or how it's being said, but also and most importantly, to what's **not** being said.*

I believe this applies 100 per cent to negotiation. The thing that your counterparty actively isn't talking about is probably the one key thing that you really should be exploring.

PART FOUR

Overcoming Obstacles

CHAPTER TEN

Objections, Lies and Emotional Responses

Negotiation is the art of turning conflict into opportunity.

As we explored earlier, for a great many people negotiation is uncomfortable. They find the whole process difficult, cringeworthy and awkward and will seek out steps to try to minimise or avoid negotiation altogether.

Learning the process is one thing. The DEALS method outlined in Part Two provides concrete steps and tools to help you prepare for your negotiations and have all of the information you need. The thing is, you can have done all your research, plotted your numbers, planned your proposals, mapped your breakpoints and understood the law ... but then something else causes us problems.

So what is it? More often than not, it's the people. The people in the negotiation and the behaviours and strategies they choose to adopt to try to get the best outcome. It is this that can often derail even the most intelligent negotiators.

Because here's the thing. Negotiation is uncomfortable to begin with, but it's even more uncomfortable when people are rude, aggressive, irrational, threatening, dismissive or rejecting, or when they talk over us, talk down to us or ignore our suggestions.

As human beings we have an inbuilt aversion to conflict. And for many people, a conflict is exactly how their negotiation might feel. Some conflicts will be small and manageable, others will be all-consuming and will swallow up the negotiation in its entirety.

In this chapter we are going to look at some of the key barriers and problems we might face at the negotiation table, as well as providing some tips for how to manage conflict when it arises.

Objections

I'm going to start this chapter by looking at objections because when my company consults with clients, inevitably one of the requests we get is to give their employees the ability to overcome objections from the other side during a negotiation.

Your counterparty might object to your opening position, they might object to your interpretation of the facts, they might object to the issues included in the deal, they might object to the location for the negotiation or they might even just object to you and how you do things. Dealing with persistent objections throughout the negotiation process can be time-consuming, exhausting and so frustrating that we would rather concede on a point just to move them on, especially when their objections seem frivolous or ungrounded based on a sensible interpretation of the facts. Of course, it is worth bearing in mind:

- The other party might interpret the facts differently to you and genuinely see their objections as valid.

- Sometimes 'negotiating by objection' is a deliberate tactic to wind you up and force concessions.

It seems that in certain industries or types of negotiation there are standard objections that come up time and time again. If you know this is true in your industry, you should of course plan in the Discover and Establish phases when you think they might make those objections and how you are going to respond to them. Alternatively, you could plan proposals that automatically address or cancel out these potential objections so it isn't viable for them to raise the objection in the first place.

If, however, you have entered into a negotiation and your counterparty is making objections constantly, on an unfounded basis or on issues that you just hadn't considered there being a potential problem with, you could try:

- Offering to explain more fully why you think their objection is invalid

- Inviting them to explain their objections more fully

- Asking for a time-out to go and consider an alternative approach

- Identifying a couple of quick and easy concessions that can help them feel 'satisfied' while you stand firm on the real issues of importance

- Changing the faces at the negotiation table

- Escalating to a higher authority.

Irrationality

'But the people I deal with are just completely irrational! There's no reasoning with them.'

Have you ever tried to negotiate with someone and grown increasingly frustrated at how irrationally they are behaving? Or become totally confused by their bizarre interpretation of the facts? Have you ever found yourself wondering why are they being so stubborn? Or thinking that what they are saying just makes no sense?

One of the most challenging situations is trying to work out how to deal with someone who seemingly won't be convinced by the evidence. How do you manage their irrational interpretations or requests and get them to behave more reasonably?

A pretty solid starting point for any negotiation is to assume that your counterparty is actually completely rational. It's probable that their behaviour is masking some other set of facts or is being used to throw us off course. When you spot what looks like 'irrational' behaviour, think about where they might be coming from. Here are a few possible scenarios:

1. Your counterparty is completely rational, you just haven't seen the world through their eyes.

In this first scenario, your counterparty's perceived irrational behaviour could be a direct result of factors in their world that are influencing their decisions and strategy that you just don't know about. Have you taken the time to consider what the realities of their situation might be? It could be that from their perspective their behaviour is completely and utterly rational. Maybe they are:

- **Uninformed:** Perhaps they haven't been given access to all of the available information or they are working from outdated figures or projections.

- **Constrained:** Perhaps they don't have full authority to negotiate on this; maybe they are constrained by lawyers, a time pressure, industry-specific regulations, budget, a colleague who is insisting on doing things a certain way, a mandate from a client?

- **Nervous:** Maybe they have had a very negative experience of a similar kind of negotiation in the past, or perhaps they are fairly new in their post and fearful of looking foolish or inexperienced?

Top Tips:
- Always take the time to think creatively about what might be going on in their world that has influenced

their handling of the negotiation. Use the Insight Locker questions to help you with this before you get to the negotiation table.

- Offer to share any current market information, industry insight, best practice, implications of deadlock, benefits gained for each side from similar agreements. This might help fill in any gaps in their knowledge and understanding and help inform their responses.

- Try directly asking them what they are trying to achieve or what the problem might be – let them know that you want to understand the issue from their perspective.

- Think about identifying some 'quick wins' that you could use to help them feel good. Is there anything that you could concede on to show willingness or to help them feel more satisfied with how the deal is going? This might help refocus the direction of travel for the deal.

2. Your counterparty is completely rational but is adopting an irrational stance to test you.

The second scenario is that your counterparty is, once again, completely rational but is adopting a seemingly irrational stance to hard bargain and to see how far they can push you on a certain point. If they have used this stance successfully with other people in the past then to them this is a completely rational strategy to adopt.

Top Tips:

- Push back. Let them know that you have limits and that you will not consider a deal on those terms.

- If that doesn't work and they persist with the irrational request, get others involved. Encourage your counterparty to bring colleagues to the meeting and bring in some of your own so that you can test your assessment of the situation.

- Capture and summarise every exchange. This can be useful later on as evidence to prove what has been going on.

- Put forward multiple proposals that provide realistic solutions to the problem – and be on record as having done this. That way your reasonable approach is documented.

- Don't make unilateral concessions – it will only encourage more of the same behaviour.

3. They are completely irrational.

So then we have the third scenario, which is that your counterparty is completely irrational and determined to work against the best interests of each side in the deal. You can test whether or not this is the case by implementing all of the tips from the previous two scenarios. If you're making no progress, the likelihood is that you are in scenario three, and the difficulty of the situation has just dramatically increased. So, how do you deal with genuine irrationality?

Top Tips:

- Don't respond in kind. Do not adopt an irrational stance of your own as it weakens your authority and credibility.

- Don't rise to it – keep your cool.

- Document everything. Keep a record of all of the attempts you have made to try to resolve the situation.

- Consider referring to a higher authority – either on their side or yours. Perhaps new faces are needed to progress this deal? Perhaps their boss isn't aware of the approach their employee has taken?

- Walk away. If the irrational behaviour continues, you might need to call off the negotiation as a signal of your strength of feeling. This may force them to ser-iously re-examine their position.

And if walking away doesn't make them re-examine their position and the deal falls through? Consider yourself lucky. Was this really the type of person that you wanted to do business with?

Anger and emotion

How do you negotiate with someone who is openly angry or emotional? What is the best way to manage someone who is upset and visibly frustrated? How should you manage their outbursts?

People tend to respond to these types of behaviours in one of two ways: they either ignore it or they react in kind.

The problem is that neither of these approaches tends to elicit the best result. By ignoring their visible distress or anger you are sending the message that you couldn't care less about them or their point of view, which is only likely to stoke the fire. Similarly, tempting as it might be to react to their angry outburst by showing your own anger, remember that this is not going to help you to refocus the negotiation on the key issues that require resolution.

Don't let their anger or emotional outbursts unsettle or distract you. Instead try the following approaches to defuse the situation.

1. Understand where this is coming from.
The best place to start is to seek to understand why they are feeling this way. The information that you gain from this will give you the insight you need to develop the right strategy to address the issue.

They might be angry because they are feeling disrespected, ignored, patronised or uninformed, or because they think that you don't take them seriously. Once you have established the reason for their anger, then seek to address it. So, if it's that they feel disrespected, let them see that you do respect them. If they feel uninformed, take steps to share information and keep them informed.

The best way to deal with the situation is to find out as much as you can about the basis for their anger. As with everything in negotiation, knowledge is power. Let them see that you take their concerns seriously and are seeking to remedy them.

2. Let them vent (in a controlled way).

A common mistake that people make when confronted with anger or emotional outbursts is to try to suppress them. They do this because they believe, rightly, that this kind of behaviour will not bring any benefit to the negotiation process or to the eventual agreement.

In an attempt to try to defuse the situation, people might use phrases such as:

> *'Shouting at each other isn't going to help anyone.'*
> *'Getting angry at me is not going to help to resolve this.'*
> *'Why don't you just take a breath and calm down?'*

On the surface they seem like sensible statements, but they can merely infuriate the angry party further as they sense that you are trying to shut them down without giving them a chance to voice their annoyance or frustration.

Instead, a recognised strategy in commercial dispute resolution and mediation is to encourage parties to voice their frustration, but in a controlled way. Don't just let them rant and rave, but do encourage them to open up about how they are feeling with probes and questions such as:

> *'I can see you are frustrated, and I want to understand why. Tell me what's going on.'*
> *'You are clearly angry about this situation, and I really want to understand why that is the case. Can you explain this to me?'*

'I would like to understand why this is causing you to be so angry. Can we talk about this?'

This helps to give legitimacy to their feelings and make them feel 'heard'. This doesn't necessarily mean that you are giving legitimacy to what they might believe, but you are acknowledging and seeking to understand why they have the feelings that they do.

3. Don't be the target.

Often the best way to protect yourself from a person's attack or outburst is to simply step out of the line of fire. Don't allow yourself to be the target by taking it personally.

Instead, recognise that their anger is a consequence of their belief or assessment of the current situation and that they are taking it out on you purely because you are the one who happens to be there in the position of counterparty.

In the midst of their anger, take a deep breath and remove yourself mentally from their line of fire. This isn't about you. This is about them. By doing this you can help to protect your own emotions and more effectively control your responses to theirs.

4. Move it on.

The final approach is one that focuses on moving your counterparty away from the elements that sparked their anger and more closely towards the underlying interests that are important to them.

After you have let them know that you take their concerns seriously by allowing them to express their opinion
and vent their frustration, you should steer them towards
achieving what mattered to them in the first place.

Questions that facilitate movement away from anger
and back to the issues on the table might include:

'What would you like the next steps to be?'
'What can we do to move this situation forward?'
*'Is there anything else we need to review before we get
back to the original issues?'*
*'Which of the issues would you like us to address first
when we get back to the table?'*

Aggression and insults

Being on the receiving end of aggression, insults and
personal slurs can be one of the most unsettling and
upsetting experiences a negotiator (or anyone for that
matter) can experience. Given the fact that negotiations
are stressful and uncomfortable anyway for most
people, this toxic combination can result in people
feeling distressed and anxious. Nobody likes to be called
names or insulted. So, what is the best way to deal with
aggression and insults if this is the strategy adopted by
the other side?

One of the most empowering ways to manage this
type of situation is to think about what might be prompt-
ing the behaviour. There is no denying that there are
some people in this world who are just quite unpleasant
and aggressive – but in most cases their behaviour comes

down to something else. Overly aggressive behaviour is frequently used to mask something that your counter-party doesn't want you to see. This might be a weakness in their position, personal vulnerabilities, pressures they are facing or desperation to get to a deal done. By acting aggressively, calling you names or being rude they are hoping to deflect from the situation and throw you off course. Their personal attacks are designed to intimidate you or to force you to react emotionally yourself.

Stay focused. There are a number of ways you can react to their behaviour, though not all of them are advisable!

1. Ignore it.

I remember when I was a kid my mum used to say to me that 'bullies bully to try to get a reaction; just ignore it'. This is wise advice that translates through to adulthood!

If your counterparty is behaving in this way, it is probably because they are hoping to prompt some kind of reaction from you. Perhaps they think you will get stressed out and lose focus, perhaps they think that you will become upset and shut down ... The point is, these behaviours are deployed to get some kind of response from you.

How about you don't give them what they are looking for? Don't react. Don't respond. Just carry on as if nothing were happening. After a while, not only are they likely to become bored of their tactics not having an impact, but they are also going to start to look ridiculous for behaving this way.

So, bite your tongue, take a breath and see how quickly they burn themselves out.

2. Respond in kind (no, not really).

Of course, there is always the temptation to respond in kind. To mirror their approach and lash out at them. Tempting as this might be, it is usually not the wise approach.

My mum also used to say 'Don't sink to their level'. Retain your cool, don't rise to it and don't reduce yourself to using tactics that undermine your credibility. Once again it seems that Mum really might know best.

3. Directly confront it and make their behaviour the issue.

I'm not suggesting that you can't be bold and challenge their behaviour. If you feel that ignoring their behaviour in some way condones it or makes you look weak, then you can take the stance of tackling it head on.

By confronting the behaviour you can defuse it, making them feel embarrassed or exposed, or simply just clearing the air to make them continuing with their strategy seem foolish and pointless.

Try asking them these questions:

- Why is the atmosphere so hostile?

- Can we all agree to try to defuse this atmosphere?

- How would you feel if you were in my shoes right now?

- Would you like me to call a break? You seem to have a lot of hostility towards me and I would like to resolve it.

- Is there anything you wish to discuss with me directly? I'm sensing you have some issue with me or the negotiation that needs to be addressed.

Liars

OK! We get it! People tell lies. The thorny and emotive issue of lying in a negotiation has already been addressed in this book in Chapter Two in relation to not assuming that people share your values.

In this section I would like you to assume that you are pretty certain you have caught a liar in the act. How do you respond?

Your response is likely to be shaped by a number of factors, including the importance of the negotiation, any ongoing relationship that needs to be preserved and the severity of the lie in question.

If we were adopting a purely morally righteous stance, the answer would of course to be that you stand up, point your finger and say: 'That is a LIE! How dare you?' But life – and business – is often a little more complicated than that. There may be implications that affect how you decide to manage the lie.

Here are two approaches on how to handle a lie from some leading practitioners in the negotiation field. They are quite different in style but offer insight into the options open to you.

Warn or confront

This is the first approach. In the 2007 book *Negotiation Genius*, Professors Malhotra and Bazerman offer up three questions to help you decide how to best respond to the lie. Their view is that, like anything in negotiation, you need to investigate the situation and understand it as fully as possible before acting upon it.

1. Was it really a lie?

So, you are pretty sure that what you have been told is a lie. However, it's still worth taking a breath and assessing whether your counterparty was actually aware that what they said was untrue. Might they be working from different information? Are they misinformed? If you decide that this is the case, you could give the benefit of the doubt, but just make sure you proceed more carefully going forward.

Malhotra and Bazerman also reference controlled negotiation studies they conducted with MBA students during which it was common for one side to claim 'but I was lied to in the negotiation!' and for their counterparty to strongly deny the accusation. What they uncovered was that typically in this instance, the accused had never actually 'spoken' a lie to the other side, but they did 'allow' the other side to be deceived or to believe information that they knew not to be true.

What should you do in this kind of situation? Will it help you to call them a liar? Or should you instead let them know that you feel you have been misled and would like to revisit a number of key issues relating to the contested point? Your actions may well be decided by your answer to the next question.

2. Do you want to continue with the negotiation?

If you become convinced that someone has deliberately lied to you, you have to make the decision either to walk away from the deal or to stay and see it through. If you are able to walk away on a matter of principle and also have nothing to lose, then there is no real issue. Of course, more often than not it won't be that straightforward. The deal might be of paramount importance for you or your business. Despite their lie you might have no choice but to continue with the negotiation. So what do you do then?

3. Do I need to warn or confront?

If you want, or need, to continue with the negotiation, you need to devise a strategy that allows you to let them know that you are aware of the lie while also giving them a chance to 'save face'. Malhotra and Bazerman assert that there are two ways you can do this. The option that you choose will depend on what it is you are seeking to achieve.

Option one: If you are not particularly upset about the lie but want to make it clear to your counterparty that they shouldn't do it in future then you can adopt a 'Warn approach'.

Warn approach

'You mentioned that the cost of the export tax is going to be the equivalent of £2.05 per unit. I think you might need to go back and have another look. We have received a number of quotes from other suppliers we have relationships with, and they have all advised the cost to be £1.85. Perhaps you are using old data or a different data set to the wider market ... but however this has happened let's all try to be really clear on the facts, figures and details going forward.'

Option two: If the lie was more substantial or problematic and you wish to receive an apology or concession in order to continue with the negotiation, then you should adopt a 'Confront approach'.

Confront approach

'You mentioned that the cost of the export tax is going to be the equivalent of £2.05 per unit. I need to let you know that we have strong relationships with other suppliers and as a result we know when someone is inflating costs. For example, we know the tax will be the equivalent of £1.85 per unit. We have been negotiating in a collaborative fashion to create more value for each side, but based on this discrepancy we are now concerned. There might be a simple reason for the differing numbers, but I just want you to know that we are disappointed with this. Can you help us

to understand your perspective and suggest some ways
we can allay our fears and wipe the slate clean?'

The Confront approach is clearly more direct and assertive, and it also implies the need for some kind of remedy
on their part. You will also notice that both options offer a
get-out clause or a chance for the offending party to save
face. This ability to save face is going to be essential if you
do wish to preserve the relationship.

Call it!

The options outlined by Malhotra and Bazerman are
what I would deem the restrained response. Susskind in
his 2014 book *Good for You, Great for Me* suggests a far
more direct and uncompromising approach.

Susskind dismisses approaches like ignoring the lie
or assuming innocence in favour of his mantra: 'Name it,
frame it, claim it'.

Name it – point out the lie.

Susskind is explicit in his desire not to leave a lie unchal-
lenged and believes that you should label the offending
statement clearly:

'That's a lie.'

Frame it – address the motive.

The next step is to say why you think it's a lie and assert
the possible motive of the person making that lie. You

should combine this with any evidence you have that contradicts their lie.

> *'That's a lie. That's not what the performance report says in section three. I can only assume your bosses are trying to devalue our claim.'*

Claim it – stand by your assertion.

Finally, you need to 'own' any statement that you are calling out as a lie. Don't do it anonymously. Don't start whispered rumours. Own your accusation.

> *'That's a lie. That's not what the performance report says in section three. I can only assume your bosses are trying to devalue our claim. The facts are actually clearly listed in the summary of section three. I would love the opportunity to meet with one of the team to discuss their inaccurate interpretation.'*

So, when it comes to lies you can choose to:

- Adopt a Warn approach
- Adopt a Confront approach
- Name it, frame it and claim it.

Whatever the situation, you should build a strategy for how to deal with lies into the Establish phase of your negotiation planning. This will allow you to appear calmer and more prepared if you are confronted with lies, rather than freaking out and floundering over what to do next.

Refusing to move

What if the other party simply keeps refusing to move? Or keeps claiming, 'Nope! That's non-negotiable!'

Frustrating as this is, you should try to keep your cool.

Don't start giving and giving

If your counterparty adopts this approach, you must resist the temptation to keep making more and more proposals, particularly if each time you do you are conceding more and more.

Are they trying to wear you down?

Standing firm is a tactic used frequently by those who assume that their counterparty will eventually grow tired of waiting and will give in to their request. Instead of doing this, you should present them with a series of reasonable proposals and ask questions as to why they are unwilling to move.

Bring on the big guns

If after a period they are still being unreasonable, you should think about referring the matter to their superior or perhaps bringing in a colleague (either yours or theirs) to witness their unreasonable behaviour.

Cut them off

If they still refuse to move and the demand they have made is something you simply cannot agree to, call a postponement, email them your latest proposal (or remind them verbally if that is preferable or your only option) and tell them that when they are ready to suggest a sensible counter-offer you will reconvene. Sometimes taking yourself out of the equation, even if only for a short time, can be very effective to force their hand.

Your own nerves, stress and anxiety

Sometimes the biggest barrier at the negotiation table is created by you. Your nerves, stress and anxiety can all combine to completely derail the negotiation.

But, you know what? Often the most empowering and useful bit of preparation you can do to limit your nerves is to remind yourself that it's not just you who finds negotiation awkward and difficult. A lot of people do and that might well include your counterparty. They might also be scared, nervous, anxious and stressed. Your counterparty is only human. As are you. They're just potentially better at keeping it under wraps than you.

CHAPTER ELEVEN

Is Negotiation a Man's Game?

'm assuming that it's already clear to you, having read the book up until this point, that I believe negotiation is as much about people and human behaviour as it is about facts, figures and processes.

It's my view that when we come to the negotiation table we make assumptions about the people we are negotiating with. Whether we like to admit to it or not, we are consciously and subconsciously influenced by a person's race, cultural background, age, experience, appearance and gender. All of these things can start to subtly impact how we perceive this person, how we expect them to behave and how we feel we might be able to interact with them.

There is a great deal of research and information out there on unconscious bias and how it can influence the decisions we make in life and in business. This is an area that is so complex and researched that I do not propose to address all of the elements of it here that relate to negotiation and deal-making. Instead, I am going to focus on one area of unconscious bias that was actually my personal catalyst for setting up my company and has helped shape my professional direction ever since.

Over the years I have developed a particular passion for and interest in the impact that gender can have at the negotiation table. This began when clients (both male and female) began asking me whether or not gender would influence the results that we might be able to achieve when negotiating. As someone who was always of the view that men and women are just as capable as each other in both business and life, I started to explore the research that had been done in this area. I spoke with academics, engaged in email exchanges with colleges and universities in Europe, the USA and Asia, and encouraged clients to give me their first-hand experiences and observations. I started to deliver talks, give advice and write on the subject and received incredibly enthusiastic feedback from both male and female clients.

However, my employers at the time took a different view and instructed me to stop looking at the issue of gender and negotiation, as in their view it would send the wrong message and be bad for business. It was my frustration at that decision, combined with the encouragement of my corporate clients, that led me to found my firm advantageSPRING, where we run popular workshops on gender at the negotiation table and don't shy away from talking about this hugely important and relevant topic.

So, to answer the question posed in the title of this

chapter: *NO. I do not believe that negotiation is a man's game. I do not believe that men have the advantage when negotiating.*

When I talk to groups of men and women on this topic the world over, I stress to them that I believe that men and women are just as capable as each other when it comes to negotiation. We are all more than capable of being amazing negotiators. I make this assertion having trained and observed men and women all over the world, in different industries, at different levels of authority, negotiating in a great number of different scenarios.

But, let's not pretend for a moment that men and women are completely the same. Let's not pretend that women don't experience different stereotypes, expectations and assumptions to those that men face.

All of this can influence how men and women are perceived in terms of their ability to negotiate, and there is plenty of research out there that evidences how some of these assumptions and stereotypes have manifested over the years.[36] Whether we like it or not, men and women are often viewed very differently as deal-makers.

Is there any use in being aware of these stereotypes?

My view is that knowledge is power. The more that we know about these possible stereotypes and differences, the more empowered we can be to challenge them and break them down. Of course, you might look at the list of stereotypes in this chapter and think that either:

- As a woman you know you don't do these things and therefore this isn't something for you to worry about; or

- As a man you are confident that you don't think this way about women and that therefore this isn't something that you need to be concerned with.

But the interesting thing about stereotypes isn't just whether you *think* that they apply to you. It's whether the decision-makers or influencers around you subconsciously think that they apply to you. It's this subconscious assumption that could lead to projects being awarded to others in the business, promotion decisions being compromised or client relationships being passed to others who they don't think will exhibit these weaknesses as negotiators.

Similarly, if you're a guy reading this and you are pretty confident that you don't fall into the trap of holding these stereotypes or of being influenced by them in your interactions with women, I would urge you to undertake a really rigorous assessment of your behaviours to see if this really is the case. Also, are the men around you guilty of perpetuating negative stereotypes – and if so, what are you going to commit to doing about it?

This chapter is all about understanding some of the differences and some of the stereotypes that exist in relation to women as negotiators. In each case I will explore the assumption, look at the research and provide guidance on how to overcome it or how to deal with it constructively.

'Women are less likely to negotiate ... and when they do, they are not ambitious enough'

In 2003, US academics Linda Babcock and Sara Laschever wrote *Women Don't Ask*. It was a ground-breaking book that looked at some of the reasons why our gender might influence the outcomes we achieve at the negotiation table. In particular, the book explored the numerous research studies which had concluded that women have a propensity to avoid negotiation or to underestimate their opportunities to do so.

A study which looked at students entering the workplace and being offered their first job discovered that only 7 per cent of women would negotiate their starting salary, compared to 57 per cent of men. This resulted in a 7.6 per cent average baseline difference ($4,000) between male and female starting salaries. Further studies (of which there are many, by the way) produced a worrying statistic that this kind of average baseline difference in salary can equate, over a career, to men earning around $1 million more than women.[37]

Research from 2003 found that when male and female students were recruited to play a board game with a researcher and were offered 'between $3 and $10' for doing so, male students were nine times more likely than female students to push back at the end of the game when everyone was routinely offered only $3. In short, the male students were being offered the $3 and saying, 'Hang on, you said between $3 and $10; I want $10', whereas the women were simply saying, 'Oh! $3! Great!'[38]

Based on the research, it certainly does appear

that women are less likely to negotiate than men. The research to back up this point is both compelling and plentiful. Of course, there are always going to be women out there who both enjoy and seek out opportunities to negotiate, but they don't seem to be the norm.

This phenomenon should be looked at on two levels:

1. Why are women less likely to negotiate?
2. Why aren't they ambitious enough when they do negotiate?

Why are women not negotiating? A well-entrenched view is that women who do 'ask', or negotiate, are often penalised by others and viewed negatively as being 'greedy, arrogant and generally not that nice'.[39] Depressingly, there is also a stack of evidence to back up the idea that women who do put themselves out there and who do ask are judged negatively by their peers. And I don't just mean male peers. Research shows us that women penalise other women in this way too.[40]

What are we missing out on by not negotiating? This is the big one isn't it? What is the implication of women avoiding negotiation? Well, unfortunately, on a personal level it can manifest itself in women missing out on promotion, salary, bonuses, high-profile projects and other opportunities they might have been able to access or benefit from. On a broader level it could result in poorer performance and outcomes when negotiating with clients, customers or suppliers. In short, there are likely to be implications from a financial, opportunity and performance perspective. As I have already said earlier in this book, negotiation is an essential part of how things get done. If women are avoiding it completely, then it follows that they are at a huge disadvantage in terms of future success and security.

Tip: Just ask! What's the worst that will happen? What's the worst that will happen if you don't?

You know what though? Not all women avoid negotiation, and a great number of us regularly engage in negotiation and take our place at the table. So what do those women who do negotiate need to be concerned about?

Evidence suggests that women who do get to the negotiation table tend not to be as ambitious with the proposals that they make. When compared with their male peers, women don't aim as high in terms of what they ask for.

- Women are more pessimistic about how much is available when they do negotiate, and so they typically ask for and get less – on average, 30 per cent less – than men.[41]

- Women report salary expectations of between 3 and 32 per cent lower than male salary expectations for the same jobs. Men expect to earn 13 per cent more than women during their first year of full-time work and 32 per cent more at their career peaks.[42]

You will know already from having read the section in Chapter Two on opening ambitiously that the extremity of our opening proposal is going to have a direct impact on where the negotiation is likely to finish. If women are routinely unambitious in what they ask for, it will have very negative implications for what they end up with. This could be in relation to salary, bonus or any term in a contract negotiation.

Pao and pay

In 2014 the interim CEO of social media company Reddit, Ellen Pao, hit headlines for banning salary negotiations at the company as a way of promoting equality. When asked why, Pao explained that because women were known to not negotiate as well as men for their salaries, she thought that removing salary negotiations would level the playing field.

While some commentators commended her approach to ensuring gender equality, others (myself included), took the completely opposite view. I viewed Pao's actions as reinforcing a very negative stereotype that women cannot negotiate as effectively as men.[43] It sets a dangerous precedent. So women can't negotiate their own salary? Probably best not to let them negotiate with customers or clients then. And while we're considering it, we should probably stop women from being managers too, as they won't be able to negotiate on behalf of or with their team members.

Surely the best thing to do if there is a perceived problem with women's ability to negotiate is to educate both the women who need to negotiate as well as those award-ing and negotiating salaries? To simply take negotiation away from women sends the wrong message and may worryingly encourage women to believe that they cannot negotiate as well as men.

Confidence

We have discussed the fact that women fear being penal-ised by their peers or boss if they negotiate, so it follows that our reluctance to open with an 'extreme' proposal or to test the water could also be driven by a fear of appear-ing unreasonable or greedy. But there may also be another reason as to why women aim far lower when approaching their negotiations.

A question of confidence? In their book *The Confidence Code*, Katty Kay and Claire Shipman explore the assertion that women are not as confident, generally, as their male peers. The book explores how societal con-ditioning and subsequent treatment can reinforce this difference and suggests ways for women to try to over-come this. In addition, the message from the authors of *Women Don't Ask* is that women routinely undervalue the assets or benefits that they personally bring to a situation.

This might start to shed light on the broader issue: of women generally undervaluing themselves. There is an old anecdote that if a man reads a job description and thinks he can do 30 per cent of the required tasks, he will consider himself suitable, whereas a women who is 80 per cent qualified will focus on the 20 per cent she can't do. Similarly, research tells us that men will take more credit than women on a project even if both have contributed equally.[44]

In the world of negotiation, if women undervalue themselves and their contributions compared to men in similar positions or of similar qualification, this could well explain why so many women don't aim high enough. We just don't think that we are worth it.

Tip: Do your research, know your value and know your market. Then, when you make the 'ask', increase it. Add on 10 per cent or 20 per cent; ask for an extra week on the deadline or for a higher percentage point on the grade. Aim high, because the guys are doing it ... and besides, you never know for sure what someone might be willing to give you.

'Women are more likely to be lied to at the negotiation table'

As we have already discussed, people lie when they negotiate. Not everyone, and not all the time, but people do. It was with great interest therefore that I read some research which suggested that women are more likely to be lied to at the negotiation table by both men *and women*.[45] Linked to this, researchers have discovered that you are more likely to be lied to if you have feminine features.[46]

But on a serious note, if it is the case that women, or anyone with feminine features, are more likely to be lied to at the negotiation table, what should we do about it? Should women adopt the stance that no one can be trusted? Should employers assume that their female negotiators might be getting poorer outcomes because their counterparties have probably fed them inaccurate information throughout?

My response is a simple one. It merely reinforces what we should already be doing as negotiators and that is being aware throughout the negotiation process that people might be lying to you, withholding information or 'bending the truth'. We should always research so thoroughly that we know our topic, market or product inside out. We should have pre-empted what we think our counterparty's positions and offers might be. We should know any governing statutes, regulations or industry best practices. In short, we should know our negotiation so well that a lie is more likely to expose itself.

We can also take steps to observe our counterparty. You can start to read your counterparty, understand some of the hidden messages in the words they use, gauge their discomfort level and look at the body language that might expose what is really going on. Every negotiator knows that you need to be prepared ... and a little bit cynical. Be ready to test what they are telling you, question anything that feels too good to be true or too draconian, listen to what they say and how they are saying it and always be ready to offer alternatives rather than anchoring to their potential lie. Effective questioning can also work to your advantage. Asking questions that force them to explain their proposition in detail or asking questions that are cleverly designed to expose contradictions or differences can put a negotiator who is bending the truth in a very tricky situation.

Final point on this? It's not just women who are lied to. Men lie to men and women lie to men too. No one is immune. So don't get complacent. Everybody, male or female, needs to wake up to the fact that not everyone will share your values ... and that includes whether or not someone might be willing to lie to you in order to get what they want.

'Women can't do the tough stuff'

I'm sure you've heard this one before. Indeed, you may have heard it touted as a positive attribute that women bring to the world of business and commerce. I'm talking about the belief that women are naturally more collaborative than men.

In Chapter Two, we discussed the fact that not all negotiations are the same. Some are more competitive in nature and some are more collaborative. It would seem logical that some people have a preference for the tougher negotiations and others for the more collaborative interactions. The danger for women (and men) arises when the decision-makers and influencers around them start to assume that they can only be effective at one or the other because of their gender.

I would certainly testify to the fact that I have met a great many women who thrive in the tougher, more direct and competitive negotiations and a great many men who seek to build partnerships and create value through collaboration. It would be very foolish of someone to sit down opposite their counterparty and make a snap judgement on their potential negotiation style solely on gender.

However, we should also not ignore the research. The tendency for women to be more collaborative in business (and in life more generally) is well documented by academics and observers from a range of backgrounds, specialisms and cultures. This is also true specifically in relation to negotiation. As I said earlier in this chapter, men and women *are* different ... it's how we understand, manage and use these differences that will set us apart.

I always think at this point it would be worth considering the idea of the Fixed Pie Bias, which asks us to consider:

> *'What proportion of the negotiations you do are inherently tough or competitive in nature?*
> *How many are win/lose transactions?*
> *How many involve people whom you will never see again and whose view of you, either personally or professionally, you don't care about at all?'*

For most people, the answer is not that many. For most people, the majority of their negotiations won't be one-off, tough, win/lose scenarios. Their negotiations are more likely to be more complex, to involve a consideration of partnership or future interaction, and to involve numerous variables and potentially numerous parties, proposals and interests.

As someone who has trained thousands of people

worldwide on effective negotiation behaviours, tools and strategies, it is certainly my view that the more collaborative negotiations are the ones that are actually more difficult to get right. The balancing of people and relationships alongside profit and commercial sustainability is a challenging one, and the notion of win/win can often be a struggle, especially if ego and a desire to win start to impact proceedings.

My own experience does seem to bear witness to the stereotype that women are more inclined to be collaborative than men and tend to actively avoid doing the tough stuff. So, for the sake of argument, let's assume that we believe the research and embrace the stereotype.

A truly collaborative mindset requires a heady blend of sophistication, maturity, professionalism, poise, creativity, curiosity and commercial expertise. So, if women are naturally more collaborative, then that's fantastic ... because it means that women are well primed to be strong all-rounders as negotiators.

Why? Because even if women are naturally more collaborative than their male peers and try to avoid doing the tough stuff, it doesn't mean that they *can't* do the tough stuff. They can. The reality is that all people are naturally competitive. We have had to be to survive and thrive as a species. The will to win and to achieve our goals exists in all of us. It's just that many of us find doing the tough stuff uncomfortable. It makes us feel awkward. It rubs up against our core values and preferences ... *but we can do it*.

We need to learn to live with this discomfort. Get

comfortable with it. Recognise that being tough, direct or competitive is often a means to an end. And remember, the other party is probably more than willing to be tough on you to ensure they walk away with what they need and leave you with a lesser outcome.

Plus, you know what? Being tough doesn't mean you have to be rude. Being direct doesn't mean you have to be aggressive. You can maintain your professionalism and integrity while being competitive and ambitious. You are more than capable of doing the tough stuff, you just have to learn how to manage your reaction to it.

'Women *really* don't like to say no'

As we have already explored, a negotiator is going to have to get used to rejection. Both delivering it and being on the receiving end of it! If every negotiation we engaged in was just littered with constant 'yeses' than my assertion would be either that you haven't got anything like the best outcome in that negotiation; or this isn't really a negotiation if you have no differences in approach, policy or practice that require you to need to seek agreement or consensus!

I don't believe that anyone likes to feel rejected, whether they're male or female. But women tend to struggle more both with hearing the word 'no' and saying it to others. Of course, in the world of negotiation where rejecting the requests of others is such an intrinsic part of the overall process, this could present some particular issues.

The process of rejection is often in itself fraught with

challenge. We are often conscious that the person we are rejecting may become angry, upset or frustrated with our decision. As a result we weigh this up and act accordingly, dependent on whether or not we need to preserve any kind of personal or professional relationship with them in the future. But even if we are going to engage with this individual on a longer term basis, there will still be requests and proposals that they make which for various reasons we will have to say no to.

Studies tell us that women are generally more concerned with the perception of others.[47] Women are more worried about not being liked and how they are viewed by the person they are interacting with. In the world of negotiation, this translates into a belief that women are likely to capitulate more quickly in a negotiation because they don't want to keep saying 'no' to their counterparty for fear of how they might be perceived.

The worry with this belief is when it starts to influence who is awarded the more difficult, challenging or high-profile deals. If decision-makers start to believe that women are less effective at saying 'no', this could have a huge knock-on effect.

Have you ever seen someone say 'no' to something, then, as an obvious result of their discomfort at having said 'no', they keep talking and talking until they have completely watered down or even cancelled out the original 'no'? This is not uncommon, but it is something that women have to learn to deal with if we are going to overcome the stereotype and secure effective and robust deals in the future.

> **How to say 'no'**
>
> When I speak with audiences around the world, I give them two alternative tips to overcome their uncomfortable relationship with the word 'no' at the negotiation table. Whichever works for you, run with it!
>
> 1.   'No' is a complete sentence.
> 2.   Rather than an abrupt 'no', try instead, 'I can't do that, but what I can do is ...'

'Women are better at negotiating for others'

For a great many people, the bulk of negotiations they undertake will be on behalf of others. Think of sporting agents, lawyers or estate agents, who negotiate on behalf of their clients, union representatives who negotiate on behalf of their members, managers who negotiate on behalf of their team, or parents who negotiate on behalf of their kids.

However there are other kinds of negotiation, in particular the kind where we are representing ourselves and our own interests. This might be in relation to salary, job title, flexible working or personal terms and conditions – anything that matters to us personally.

According to research, it is these kind of negotiations where women have a real problem.[48] In short, women are far more effective at negotiating for others than they are for themselves.

This idea is very well entrenched and robustly researched. Numerous reasons have been put forward as to why women won't negotiate as hard for themselves as they would for the people around them but they tend to boil down to two key issues which are: a fear of how they will be perceived; and a chronic undervaluing of skills and worth.

The first issue links back to a theme that appears to run throughout this chapter, which is that women are often socially penalised for asserting themselves and asking for what they want. The problem is heightened by the fact that women are often very aware of this and are conscious of the possible or perceived ramifications.

The second links back to the notion mentioned earlier that women tend to have lower levels of confidence than men. They more frequently downplay their achievements, underestimate the impact of their contributions and undervalue themselves and their skills. As a result they ask less frequently and ask for less.

These two limiting issues combined might explain why women appear to achieve better outcomes for others than they do for themselves: when advocating for someone else you can throw all of your energy and skills behind 'selling' the achievements and value of that individual. It ceases to be a personal matter and so the notion of being arrogant, greedy or overly ambitious does not impair the negotiation.

Once again, whether or not we believe this stereotype or belief to be true on a personal level, the volume of the research evidence means that we would be foolish to ignore it.

I always give two pieces of advice to the women that I

speak to. If you recognise that you might be selling your-self short at the negotiation table, I would encourage you to follow either of these two strategies, the first from Margaret Neale and the second from Lois Frankel.

The first approach is to embrace it ... and use it! Professor Margaret Neale of Stanford University is a leading expert on the psychology of bargaining and on the impact of gender on negotiation. Neale is an expert on the topic of how women can become more effective nego-tiators and has also contributed to learning resources for women as part of the Lean In campaign, the movement set up by Sheryl Sandberg to encourage women to speak up and 'lean in' in the workplace.[49]

Neale's advice is to use the fact that we negotiate bet-ter for others to our advantage. She feels that if this is the case, we should use it to make sure we end up with bet-ter outcomes. I always refer to this advice from Professor Neale as her 'Husband, Horses and Chickens' advice.

The thrust of the message is that if we recognise that we are better at negotiating for others, before we next have to negotiate on a very personal issue, such as salary or flexible working, we should remind ourselves of all of the people who are depending on us to get a great result. So, Neale says that before she would go and negotiate anything with the dean of her faculty she would remind herself of all of those relying on her. It might sound some-thing like this:

'Come on Margaret. At home you've got a husband, two sons, three daughters, two grandkids, two dogs, a

cat and eight chickens ... as well as a mortgage to pay.
You'd better get a good result here.'

I know from experience that some women *love* Professor Neale's approach. As soon as they hear it they embrace it fully, and a great many have contacted me at a later date saying how well it has worked for them. But I also know that some women find the advice slightly uncomfortable, as it appears to suggest that a woman's worth needs to be gauged by the people around her, rather than being based on her own contribution, skillset or value.

So as an alternative, I also give my female audiences some advice that was given to me by Dr Lois Frankel, author of the groundbreaking 2004 book *Nice Girls Don't Get the Corner Office*. Right before I went to New York in 2015 to do a speaking tour on the topic 'Is Negotiation a Man's Game?' I sent a tweet to Dr Frankel asking for the one piece of advice she would give to women who want to improve as negotiators. Her reply was succinct (of course, it had to be in 140 characters!) but the gist was that as women 'we need to recognise that we are worth it' and we should 'learn to view advocating for ourselves as both admirable and acceptable'.

Now this will potentially be the more challenging of the two approaches. It will require confidence, practice, tackling your nerves, being expertly prepared and knowing how to deal with anxiety, stress and the impulse to back down too easily. But in my view that's something that most negotiators should be learning how to do anyway. Male or female!

I always say to my audiences, explore which of these approaches works for you, then use it. If the outcome of adopting either of these strategies is that you end up with a more robust outcome for yourself, then my job here is done!

'Women don't like to be chameleons'

The final stereotype or belief that I want to highlight is one that, again, I believe both men and women struggle with when they are negotiating. As I said in the Common Negotiation Mistakes chapter, we need to be able to flex and adapt our style as negotiators. This is because not all negotiations are the same; each will require different strategies, tactics and behaviours in order to get the optimum outcome.

One of the overwhelming pieces of feedback I have received from both men and women across the globe is that women generally feel more uncomfortable about flexing and adapting their behavioural style at work than men do. Women report that they find it disingenuous and inauthentic, or they worry that it will be obvious to their counterparty that they are just 'acting' and will therefore lose their professional credibility. Men just don't seem to have this level of concern with having to play tough when it suits them.

Of course, one of the reasons for this could be the 'social penalty' that women experience when they do have to behave in ways that might fall outside of the traditional female behavioural set.[50] As stated previously, when women are seen to be tough, direct or assertive, it can elicit a negative response from both men and women. To avoid eliciting this reaction, many women therefore avoid deviating from a more 'feminine' way of behaving.

Whatever the reason, we have heard from many women that they do not believe that changing their behavioural style will work in their favour.

Once again, I believe that we must challenge this. To be able to adapt your behaviour and style in a professional and credible way is a key component of being an amazing negotiator. If you can't be tough on a difficult issue when the situation requires it or can't build rapport and partnership when required then you are essentially a one-trick pony.

I believe that negotiators should be more than able to adapt their approach in a manner that is professional, credible, convincing and authentic. Not only that, my view is actually that women have the distinct advantage in being able be flexible in this way. Why? Because we have been doing it for generations. Women have always been required to play multiple roles. This has been especially true since women won the vote and entered the workplace.

I will use myself as an example. Over the course of a week or a month I will play a number of different roles. So, I know that the Natalie who had a few too many glasses of Rioja with her friends in a bar in Brighton the other week (and was slightly talkative and exuberant!) is very different to the Natalie who was forced into getting up at 3.30am every day by her toddler, and who tried to reason with him that this was not a sensible time to have breakfast. And that Natalie is very different to the Natalie who led tough negotiations in France with a very direct trade union official. And that Natalie is again very different to the one who coached a concerned CEO on the phone about a forthcoming merger and the impact it would have on the emotional well-being of his staff.

Each situation resulted in a very different version of Natalie, exhibiting different behaviours and approaches. But they were all still Natalie. I never stopped being Natalie for one minute. I have just got comfortable with the fact that life requires us to be flexible. To have multi-faceted versions of ourselves that we use at different times.

That's not disingenuous. That's not misleading. That's just a sensible approach to dealing with everything that life throws at us.

CHAPTER TWELVE

It's a Cultural Thing

'Culture is the collective programming of the mind that distinguishes one category of people from another.'
– Geert Hofstede

As business evolves, technology advances, and new markets open up, it is clear for all to see that we are living and working in a global economy. As a result, it is not uncommon for us to have to negotiate with people from different countries and continents. This might be negotiating with one of our colleagues from a regional office or negotiating a supply deal with a company on the other side of the world. For most of us, at some point in our career we will have to contend with negotiating across borders.

My firm trains teams in large companies all over the world on how to negotiate effectively. We are regularly asked what impact culture can have on a negotiation. The short answer is that, of course, the culture can have a huge impact on the deals you do. But our advice is always not to become intimidated or too obsessed by it. As with everything in negotiation, awareness and knowledge is power.

In this chapter, I outline some of the things you might want to consider before negotiating across cultures, followed by a list of the aspects you should *always* remember when negotiating across cultures.

What you might want to consider

The following outlines just a few of the things you might want to consider when you are starting to think about negotiating across cultures. This list is by no means exhaustive, but I hope it can stimulate some thinking to help you when you negotiate.

There are collective differences across cultures

In his definitive text, *When Cultures Collide: Leading across cultures,* Richard D. Lewis outlines the fact that the world's cultures are vast and diverse. However, he offers a classification to assist the global business executive with navigating some of the common differences and similarities between our numerous cultures. He splits world cultures into three main categories of cultural personality traits.

Linear-actives: those who plan, schedule, organise and do one thing at a time.

Lewis suggests that Germans and Swiss fall into this group.

Common traits: introverted, patient, quiet, private, punctual, job-oriented, sticks to plans, sticks to facts, dislikes losing face, separates the social from the professional.

Multi-actives: people who are lively and like to do many things at once; they plan their priorities based on thrill or the importance attached to each task.

He asserts that Italians, Latin Americans and Arabs fall into this group.

Common traits are: extroverted, impatient, inquisitive, talkative, not punctual, changes plans, people-oriented, seeks favours, expressive, interweaves the social and the professional.

Reactives: cultures that prioritise courtesy and respect, listening calmly and quietly, and reacting carefully to each side's view or proposal.

He asserts that the Chinese, Japanese and Finns are in this group.

Common traits are: introverted, patient, respectful, good listener, reactive, people-oriented, thoughtful, plans slowly, uses controlled body language, connects the social and the professional.

Understanding some of the generalities that exist across cultures can help you to begin your planning and preparation. The Linear/Multi/Reactive model (LMR) developed by Lewis is a great starting point for thinking about how best to communicate, provide information, present proposals and plan ahead for the duration and style of the impending negotiation. For example, Lewis explores how different cultures best like to receive information, with those from Multi-active cultures preferring to engage in exploratory dialogue, and those from Linear-active cultures preferring to receive hard data. This might help you to work out a strategy as to how best to present your proposals to the other side, or how best to reason with them if they reject your request or point of view.

Consider the social setting

You should be aware that different cultures view the negotiation process differently. Some cultures will view it as a straightforward and pragmatic exchange of information that sits firmly within their professional sphere, whereas others will view it as a social ceremony in which there are specific considerations in relation to participants, hospitality and protocol. Some cultures view it as a formal and more public process by which to ceremonially ratify a series of decisions already made behind closed doors, whereas others view the negotiation process as an opportunity to unpack and explore the possibilities that might be possible.

Learn body language norms

Different cultures have varying interpretations of body language, such as facial expressions, physical contact, eye contact, hand gestures and what we do with our feet. There are also differing norms in terms of personal space. Do your research to avoid any awkwardness.

Language barriers exist within languages

This isn't referring to the fact that different countries speak different languages and therefore an interpreter may be required. It refers instead to the fact that even within languages there can be varying nuances and interpretations that can have a huge impact. While English is often viewed as the international language of diplomacy and trade, it should be noted that words and phrases such as 'fair', 'reasonable', 'level playing field' and 'makes business sense' will have different meanings across different cultures.

Understanding decision-making

In many ways negotiation is simply the means and process of reaching a decision or series of decisions. How decisions are made can vary from culture to culture. There will be differences as to how long it will take to make a decision, who will be involved, whose opinion carries more weight and how binding a 'final' decision really is.

Social taboos

Different taboos exist in every country in the world. In Lewis's book, he reveals the following: in Russia it is taboo to stand with your hands in your pockets. In Indonesia it is taboo for your head to be higher than that of a more senior person. In England it is considered taboo to overtly discuss your successes or strengths. In Malaysia it is taboo to point with your index finger. While some of them might appear outdated or outlandish from your perspective, you would be wise to adhere to them where possible. Or at least take the time to discover from those with more understanding of the culture whether they are taken seriously. This is because many taboos are deeply rooted in history, religion or societal belief and to ignore them can send a strong message of disrespect.

Remember
The process of negotiation is universal
It is worth remembering that negotiation as both a concept and a process is pretty universal. Human beings have been negotiating with each other since the dawn of civilisation. It acts as a social lubricant that allows relationships to grow, agreements to be made, goods to be traded, communities to function and countries to collaborate. The key elements of the process of negotiation (trading, persuading, influencing, seeking an agreement, securing an outcome) are consistent in countries and cultures around the world.

The point here is that the process of negotiation that you embark on with someone in a different continent to you is not going to be radically different from a negotiation with someone based down the street. So don't panic. You will still need to do your research, make some proposals, hear their proposals, experience rejection and try to reach some kind of agreement. All of that stuff doesn't fundamentally change. It should be standard that before any negotiation you have taken the time to explore anything that could well impact how the deal unfolds. This could include market conditions, past performance, the balance of power, financial implications, reputational issues, corporate aspiration and potentially culture. What might change though is some of the stuff around that process, and this is where knowledge is power.

Do your research

Of course, having just said that negotiation is universal, the rituals and behaviours that different cultures bring to a negotiation can be quite different. While this doesn't impact the fundamental *process* of negotiation it will almost certainly impact your *experience* of a negotiation.

There are some pretty well-established and understood differences that exist in relation to how different cultures approach negotiation. This might be in relation to the hierarchy required not to offend your counterparty, the length of time taken to consider your proposals, the level of toughness adopted, the offence that might be taken at an extreme offer, whether they wish to get to know you or just get straight down to business, or whether or not women are welcomed at the negotiation table. We call these cultural nuances, and they might well impact your experience of deal-making.

If you have identified that a difference in culture might impact your deal, then just as with any other influencing factor, you have a duty to research it thoroughly in order to mitigate its impact and ensure you are fully prepared. There are lots of places that you can gain information on cultural differences, including speaking to colleagues based in or with experience in that region, researching online, or reading books such as Richard D. Lewis's.

But don't assume

Of course, while knowledge is power, it is also essential that we don't fall into the trap of assuming that cultural stereotypes are universally true. Some deal-makers will indeed adhere to cultural norms or fit common national stereotypes. However, for many others they could not be further from the truth. My firm trains negotiators around the world, and I can testify that I have met many people who certainly don't match up to those stereotypes. I also know a great many British negotiators closer to home who are not at all governed by fairness!

A clever negotiator should seek to understand what the cultural norms are so that they can prepare for them *if and when* they are presented with them. The danger is that we read the stereotype and then automatically assume that our counterparty will exhibit it or respond to it. Awareness rather than assumption has to be the key to effective preparation. This all boils down to the fact that people negotiate with people, and ultimately people are all different.

Preparing for cultural difference

It is worth remembering that stereotypes and social conventions exist for a reason: on a societal level they act as points of reference for interacting with strangers. But we must learn to manage them and utilise correctly and not be led astray by lazy assumptions.

It is essential that you research and understand how culture *could* result in the negotiation being conducted differently or how the other party might behave because of where they come from, but it is just as important to remember that everyone is different. Treat each negotiation and each negotiator individually, and be prepared for anything!

PART FIVE

Tools and Further Reading

Negotiation Tactics: Reference Guide

E arlier in the book I said that knowledge is power when deal-making. The following reference guide is designed to help you identify some of the common tactics that are used in negotiations. Some of these tactics, such as time-outs, conveying disbelief and using silence will stand you in good stead and may be a useful addition to your negotiation toolkit.

However, I am not advocating that you should look to use all of these tactics, as many are fairly aggressive, intimidating and potentially counter-productive. As we identified earlier in the book, sometimes people will deliberately try to intimidate you, trick you and manipulate you in order to get a result that works in their favour. Throughout the book we have looked at ways to combat this, particularly in Chapter Ten. As well as following that advice, you can also refer to this guide to gain some insight into some of the tactics that people might use against you.

Consider how each tactic might be used against you ... or why you might consider using it.

Ambush!

Showing up at a negotiation as a large group and out-numbering the opposition can have a significant impact in terms of conveying power as well as potentially intimidating your counterparty. How you then proceed to behave as a large group will dictate how this tactic will be received by the other side.

Bullying

Using inappropriate, insulting or unpleasant behaviour such as shouting, screaming, swearing or gesturing to intimidate the other side. If you are on the receiving end of this remember that there are ways to defuse this behaviour, and uncovering the reasons why they are doing it could actually work in your favour.

The decoy

By placing great emphasis on something that you don't actually want and which is unachievable for the other side to give, you place yourself in a potentially stronger position to get them to agree to the things that do really matter to you. This will require effective planning in order to execute it, as you will need to understand what each side could potentially concede on and to what degree. You might also have to carry out some preconditioning to sow the seed with your counterparty that the decoy variable matters to you.

Appeal to their ego

Using phrases and questions such as 'Are you sure you have the authority to agree to this?' or 'I'm not sure whether your firm is open to this kind of innovative approach' can serve to trigger the other side's ego. If they value hierarchy and power, they might go to greater lengths to show you that they are mandated to make a decision or that they can authorise a different approach, even if it hadn't originally been part of their plan to do so.

It's up to you

Be cautious when your counterparty offers you the choice of two options in a challenging negotiation. An often used tactic to try to make you feel like you are in control is for your counterparty to offer you the freedom to choose between two options – but each option is as bad as the other, just dressed up differently. Always consider the impact of any concession you make.

Seriously? Come on!

By conveying disbelief at your counterparty's point of view or proposal you might be able to embarrass them into making a further move or rethinking completely.

Time-out

Adjourning the negotiation to take stock, review progress, craft new proposals or simply let each side reflect or calm down can be incredibly useful. Time-outs can vary in length and can result in renewed focus for all sides. A well-timed time-out can also prevent deadlock.

Do be mindful of your counterparty using time-outs excessively to try to increase time pressure on you or to avoid talking about key or contentious issues.

Could you just explain to me ...

By playing dumb and asking the right questions you can assess your counterpart's honesty and how much information they might have access to. If you ask a question to which you already know the answer you are able to assess their integrity.

Too good to be true

The old saying 'If something is too good to be true, it probably is' should be remembered when at the negotiating table. If an offer seems to be too good to be true, actively look for hidden disadvantages or issues that might not be immediately obvious.

I'll need to speak to ...

Telling your counterparty that you need to defer to a higher authority before coming to an agreement can be a great way to prevent yourself being backed into a corner and agreeing to something you don't really think you should. It can also help preserve or improve your relationship with the other side as you can 'blame' certain decisions on someone other than you or seem like the 'hero' when you 'persuade' the higher authority to agree to something in your counterpart's favour.

Let's get physical

Be aware that some counterparts will seek to unsettle you using physical means such as invading your personal space, positioning chairs in such a way that you are isolated or even doing things unexpectedly such as putting their feet up on the table. This is often done to throw you off guard or give the impression that they are more powerful than you.

It's oh-so quiet

When faced with a wall of silence most of us will go to great lengths to fill it. A clever negotiator knows that sometimes saying nothing can encourage the other side to keep making concessions rather than sit out the silence. Be mindful of this happening to you and make sure you don't keep making concession after concession. If they keep saying nothing, ask them a question or state that you 'would be keen to hear their views'.

Can we take this off the record?

A chance to explore options with your counterparty, air your concerns or share some insight, an off-the-record meeting can be a great tactic to keep your negotiation on track. Just ensure that it is truly off the record and agree some ground rules if you are discussing things that are particularly sensitive. You don't want your 'off the record' discussions being used against you in a more formal setting.

I wouldn't do this for everyone

Leading your counterparty to believe that you have gone to great lengths to facilitate something for them that is exceptional and above standard practice can lead them to feel indebted to you and more likely to agree to your requests.

Good cop, bad cop

When one of the negotiating team plays the good guy and the other the bad guy. The bad guy is aggressive, dismissive and rude, and then they are taken out of the equation for a while by the good guy. This is designed to make you feel indebted to the good guy so that you more readily agree to their suggestions. If you are on the receiving end of it, just remember to stick to your plan and remember that they are playing a game. Don't fall for it. If you are looking to use this tactic, ensure that your bad guy is credible, and don't go over the top with this. Otherwise you end up looking like a comedy villain and the tactic becomes transparent.

Everyone else is doing it

Showing your counterparty evidence that everyone else in their industry is buying this product or doing it this way can create a sense of panic about being the odd ones out or miss out on best practice.

Can you match your competitors?

A common tactic is for one side to point out to the other that one of their competitors has offered a far better proposal. You are pushed to see if you can match it and, out of fear of losing the deal, you do, even though the outcome becomes far less profitable. Be clear on your breakpoints and don't agree to things that are damaging for you. Also make sure you ask for evidence or detail of the competitor's proposal; that way you can point out why your proposal is different/better/more robust. It can also help you establish whether the proposal from your competitor even exists.

Tick-tock

> *'Come on! I've got to go in five minutes. Do we have a deal?'*
> *'You have until the end of the day to make a decision.'*
> *'If I don't hear by Monday I will be speaking to another provider.'*

When your counterparty uses deadlines to try to force an agreement from you, make sure you find time to consider fully the implications. Try not to be rushed into anything.

Further Reading

Adler, Robert S., & Elliot M. Silverstein, 'When David Meets
    Goliath: Dealing with power differentials in negotiations',
    Harvard Negotiation Law Review, Vol. 5, 2000.

Ariely, Dan, *Predictably Irrational: The hidden forces that shape
    our decisions*, HarperCollins, 2010.

Babcock, Linda, & Sara Laschever, *Women Don't Ask:
    Negotiation and the gender divide*, Princeton University
    Press, 2003.

Bazerman, Max H., & Dolly Chugh, *Bounded Awareness:
    Focusing failures in negotiation*, Psychological Press, 2004.

Bazerman, Max H., & Margaret A. Neale, 'Heuristics in
    negotiation: Limitations to effective dispute resolution',
    in *Negotiating in Organisations*, M.H. Bazerman & R.J.
    Lewicki (Eds), Sage, 1983.

Benoliel, Michael, & Wei Hua, *Negotiating (Essential Managers
    Series)*, Dorling Kindersley, 2015.

Cialdini, Robert B., *Influence: The psychology of persuasion*,
    HarperCollins, 2007.

Collins, Patrick, *Negotiate to Win*, Sterling Publishing, 2009.

Dobelli, Rolf, *The Art of Thinking Clearly*, Hodder &
    Stoughton, 2013.

Eggert, Max, *Brilliant Body Language*, Pearson Education, 2010.

Forsyth, Patrick, *The Negotiator's Pocketbook*, Alresford
    Press, 1993.

Frankel, Lois P., *Nice Girls Don't Get the Corner Office: 101 unconscious mistakes women make that sabotage their careers*, Time Warner Book Group, 2004.

Harvard Business Review on Winning Negotiations, Harvard Business School Press, 2011.

Horton, Simon, *Negotiation Mastery*, MX Publishing, 2012.

Johnston, Peter D., *Negotiating with Giants: Get what you want against the odds*, Negotiation Press, 2012.

Kennedy, Gavin, *Negotiation: An A-Z Guide*, Profile Books, 2009.

Kolb, Deborah M., & Judith Williams, *The Shadow Negotiation*, Simon & Schuster, 2000.

Lax, David A., & James K. Sebenius, *3D Negotiation*, Harvard Business School Press, 2006.

Malhotra, Deepak, & Max H. Bazerman, *Negotiation Genius*, Bantam Dell, 2008.

Morley, Iain, *The Devil's Advocate*, Third Edition, Thomson Reuters, 2015.

Neale, Margaret, & Thomas Lys, *Getting (More of) What You Want*, Profile Books, 2015.

Poundstone, William, *Priceless: the hidden psychology of value*, Oneworld Publications, 2014.

Raiffa, Howard, *The Art and Science of Negotiation*, Belknap Press, 1985.

Susskind, Lawrence, *Good for You, Great for Me*, PublicAffairs, 2014.

Thompson, Leigh, *The Truth about Negotiations*, Second Edition, FT Press, 2013.

Wheeler, Michael, *The Art of Negotiation*, Simon & Schuster, 2015.

Endnotes

1. I will refer throughout this book to the 'negotiation table', although of course, not all negotiations are conducted face to face, at a table. In today's global economy, a great many deals are played out virtually using email, phones, online submission systems and web conferencing. Please assume that when I talk about the 'negotiation table', I'm referring to negotiation in its broadest sense.

2. Galinsky, Seiden, Kim & Medvec, 'The Dissatisfaction with Having Your First Offer Accepted', *Personality and Social Psychology Bulletin* 28, 2002, 271–83.

3. Ritov, 'Anchoring in Simulated Competitive Negotiation', *Organizational Behavior and Human Decision Processes*, Vol. 67, No. 1, 1996.

4. Northcraft & Neale, 'Experts, Amateurs and Real Estate: An anchoring and adjustment perspective on property pricing decisions', *Organizational Behavior and Human Decision Processes*, 84, 1987.

5. Poundstone, *Priceless: the hidden psychology of value*, Oneworld Publications, 2014.

6. Chapman & Bornstein, 'The More You Ask for, the More You Get: Anchoring in personal injury verdicts', *Applied Cognitive Psychology*, 10, 1996.

7. Tversky & Kahneman, 'Judgement under Uncertainty: Heuristics and biases', *Science* 185, 1974.

    The research used a carnival-style spinning wheel of fortune marked with numbers 1 to 100. However, the wheel was rigged to only stop at 10 or 65. Participants were then asked two questions: 'Is the percentage of African nations in the UN higher or lower than [the number that came up on the wheel]?' 'What is the percentage of African nations in the UN?' The research discovered that whatever number participants had been subjected to on the wheel hugely influenced their answers to the questions. That is, if the number on the wheel was 10, the average percentage number given to the second question was 25 per cent. Whereas if the number they saw on the wheel was 65, the average answer was 45 per cent.

8.   Galinsky, Seiden, Kim & Medvec, 'The Dissatisfaction'.

9.   Baumeister, Finkenauer & Vohs, 'Bad Is Stronger than Good', *Review of General Psychology* 5 (4), 2001, 323–70.

10.   Of course, the second part of her statement was that if you *do* ask, you might be penalised for it. In Chapter Eleven, I explore research which shows that, unfortunately, women *are* often perceived more negatively for negotiating than men. This doesn't change my position that we still need to ask; we just need to think creatively about how we do it.

11.   Jaccard, 'Objectives and Philosophy of Public Affairs Education' in *Increasing Understanding of Public Problems and Policies: A group study of four topics in the field of extension education*, Farm Foundation, 1956, 12.

12.   Susskind, *Good for You, Great for Me*, PublicAffairs, 2014.

13.   Adler & Silverstein, 'When David Meets Goliath: Dealing with power differentials in negotiations', *Harvard Negotiation Law Review*, Vol. 5, 2000.

14.   Adler & Silverstein, 'David Meets Goliath'.

15.   Adler & Silverstein, 'David Meets Goliath'.

16. Fisher & Ury, *Getting to Yes: Negotiating an agreement without giving in*, Random House Business, 2012, first edition 1981.

17. Susskind, *Good for You.*

18. Greenpeace, 'Caught Red-Handed: How Nestlé's use of palm oil is having a devastating impact on rainforest, the climate and orang-utans', 17 March 2010. http://www.greenpeace.org/international/en/publications/reports/caught-red-handed-how-nestle/

19. https://www.change.org/impact

20. Adler & Silverstein, 'David Meets Goliath'.

21. Simon and Thaler's work is explored in Bazerman & Chugh's 'Bounded Awareness' in *Frontiers of Social Psychology: Negotiations*, L. Thompson (Ed.), Psychological Press, 2005.

22. Simon, *Reason in Human Affairs.* Stanford University Press, 1983.

23. Lerner & Tiedens, 'Portrait of the Angry Decision Maker: How appraisal tendencies shape angers influence on cognition' *Journal of Behavioural Decision Making* 19, No. 2, 2006.

24. Bazerman & Chugh, 'Bounded Awareness: Focusing problems in negotiation' in Thompson, L. (Ed.), *Frontiers of Social Psychology: Negotiations*. Psychology Press, 2005; Chugh & Bazerman, 'Bounded Awareness: What you fail to see can hurt you' in *Mind and Society*, 6 (1), 2007, 1–18.

25. Various:
Bazerman, Magiozzi & Neale, 'The Acquisition of an Integrative Response in a Competitive Market', *Organizational Behavior and Human Decision Processes*, 35 (3), 1985.
Tsay & Bazerman, 'A Decision-making Perspective to Negotiation: A review of the past and a look into the future', Harvard University working paper, 2009.

Bazerman & Chugh, 'Bounded Awareness: Focusing failures in negotiation', Harvard University working paper, 2003.

26. Tversky & Kahneman, 'The Framing of Decisions and the Psychology of Choice', *Science* 211, 1981.

27. Bazerman, Magliozzi & Neale, 'Integrative Bargaining in a Competitive Market', *Organizational Behaviour and Human Decision Processes*, 35 (3), 1985.

28. Bazerman & Neale, 'Heuristics in Negotiation: Limitations to effective dispute resolution', in *Negotiating in Organisations*, Bazerman & Lewicki (Eds), Sage, 1983; Thompson & Hastie, 'Social Perception in Negotiation', *Organizational Behavior and Human Decision Processes*, 47, 1990, 98–123.

29. Cialdini, *Influence: The psychology of persuasion*, HarperCollins, 2007. First edition published 1984.

30. As cited in Cialdini, *Influence*.

31. As cited in Cialdini, *Influence*.

32. Valley, Moag & Bazerman, 'A Matter of Trust: Effects of communication on the efficiency and distribution of outcomes' *Journal of Economic Behaviour and Organisations*, 34, 1998.

33. Langer, Blank & Chanowitz, 'The Mindlessness of Ostensibly Thoughtful Action: The role of placebic information in interpersonal interaction', *Journal of Personality and Social Psychology*, 36, 1978.

34. Mehrabian & Wiener, 'Decoding of Inconsistent Communications', *Journal of Personality and Social Psychology*, 6 (1), May 1967, 109–14. Also Mehrabian & Ferris, 'Inference of Attitudes from Nonverbal Communication in Two Channels', *Journal of Consulting Psychology*, Vol. 31 (3), June 1967, 248–52.

35. Willis & Todorov, 'First Impressions: Making up your mind after a

100-Ms exposure to a face', *Psychological Science*, Vol. 17 (7), July 2006, 592–98.

36. Babcock & Laschever, *Women Don't Ask: Negotiation and the gender divide*, Princeton University Press, 2003.

37. Babcock & Laschever, *Women Don't Ask*.

38. Small, Babcock, Gelfand, Gettman, 'Who Goes to the Bargaining Table? The influence of gender and framing on the initiation of negotiation', *Journal of Personality and Social Psychology*, Vol. 93, No. 4, 2007, 600–13.

39. Bowles, Babcock & Lai, 'Social Incentives for Gender Differences in the Propensity to Initiate Negotiations: Sometimes it does hurt to ask', *Organizational Behaviour and Human Decision Processes*, 2006.

40. Bowles, Babcock & Lai, 'Social Incentives'.

41. Babcock & Laschever, *Women Don't Ask*.

42. Babcock & Laschever, *Women Don't Ask*.

43. I wrote an article on LinkedIn on the topic: 'My Problem with Pao and Pay', 8 April 2015. https://www.linkedin.com/pulse/my-problem-pao-pay-natalie-reynolds

44. Haynes & Heilman, 'It Had to Be You (Not Me)!: Women's attributional rationalization of their contribution to successful joint work outcomes', *Personality and Social Psychology Bulletin*, 7 May 2013.

45. Kray, Kennedy & Van Zant, 'Not Competent Enough to Know the Difference? Gender stereotypes about women's ease of being misled predict negotiator deception', *Organizational Behavior and Human Decision Processes*, Vol. 125 (2), November 2014, 61–72.

46. Gladstone & O'Connor, 'A Counterpart's Feminine Face Signals Cooperativeness and Encourages Negotiators to Compete',

Organizational Behavior and Human Decision Processes, Vol. 125 (1), September 2014, 18–25.

47. Kay & Shipman, *The Confidence Code: The science and art of self-assurance – What women should know,* HarperBusiness, 2014.

48. Bowles, Babcock & McGinn, 'Constraints and Triggers: Situational mechanics of gender in negotiation', *Journal of Personality and Social Psychology,* Vol. 89 (6), December 2005, 951–65.

49. You can find Neale's video and accompanying discussion guide on the Lean In education site: 'Learn a simple framework for approaching negotiation in a whole new light'. http://leanin.org/education/negotiation/

50. Bowles, Babcock & Lai, 'Social Incentives'.

At advantageSPRING we believe that anyone can learn to be a brilliant negotiator. Our approach to negotiation is to demystify it: to make it accessible and understandable for everyone.

The advantageSPRING team works with clients around the world to provide interactive negotiation workshops and coaching and advisory services that boost confidence and capability and that directly result in enhanced commercial results.

We have partnered with banks, law firms, manufacturers, retailers, technology firms, government departments, international development agencies, media organisations and leading academic institutions. Our training is challenging, enjoyable and memorable – and, most importantly, it works.

advantageSPRING

We know negotiation

To find out more about advantageSPRING,
visit **www.advantagespring.com**
Email us at office@advantagespring.com

@AdvSpring
@AdvSpringCEO

 advantageSPRING

Acknowledgements

Anyone who has written a book will know that it can be a challenging, frustrating and laborious process at times! I would like to thank the following people for supporting me during the writing of *We Have a Deal*, whether through giving advice, offering constructive criticism, believing in me and my approach, or simply just being brilliant.

Colleagues and collaborators:
Hayley Capstick (my patient, long-suffering and outstanding PA), John Viner-Smith, Devon Smiley, Karen Wrethman, Steve Broach, Sally Davidson, Eiren O'Keefe, Zara Shirwan, Harriet Minter, Debra Ward, Simon Roche, Vanessa Vallely, Samantha McClary, Doris Braun, Sarka Hildon, Sue Beavil, Fotini Iconomopoulos, Graham Allcott, Imelda Wright, Davo Ruthven-Stuart, Phillip Westermeyer, Valerie Hogan, Joy Lo Dico, Alison Challis, Zoe Layden, Marty Rolle, Yvonne Smyth, Abi Colthrust, Yvonne Smith and Fiona McKay.

Special mentions to:
Kiera Jamison
Chaz Allcott and Varsha Chilka
Alex Lee
Sally Hendrup-Smith
Sue Reynolds
Ashley and Celia Pace
Diane and Steve Lee
Jonny Pace and Michelle Clarke
Chris Pace and Ben Looker

My fantastic, supportive and inspiring mum, Dawn Pace

And finally to my wonderful husband, Chris Reynolds, and amazing little boy, Leo. You are both unbelievably awesome.